D1451690

AUNTY ACID'S

OFFICE

MANUAL

GIBBS SMITH
TO ENRICH
AND INSPIRE
HUMANKIND

WHEN I WAS FIRST APPROACHED TO WRITE AN **OFFICE SURVIVAL GUIDE**, I SAID, **"NO!"**

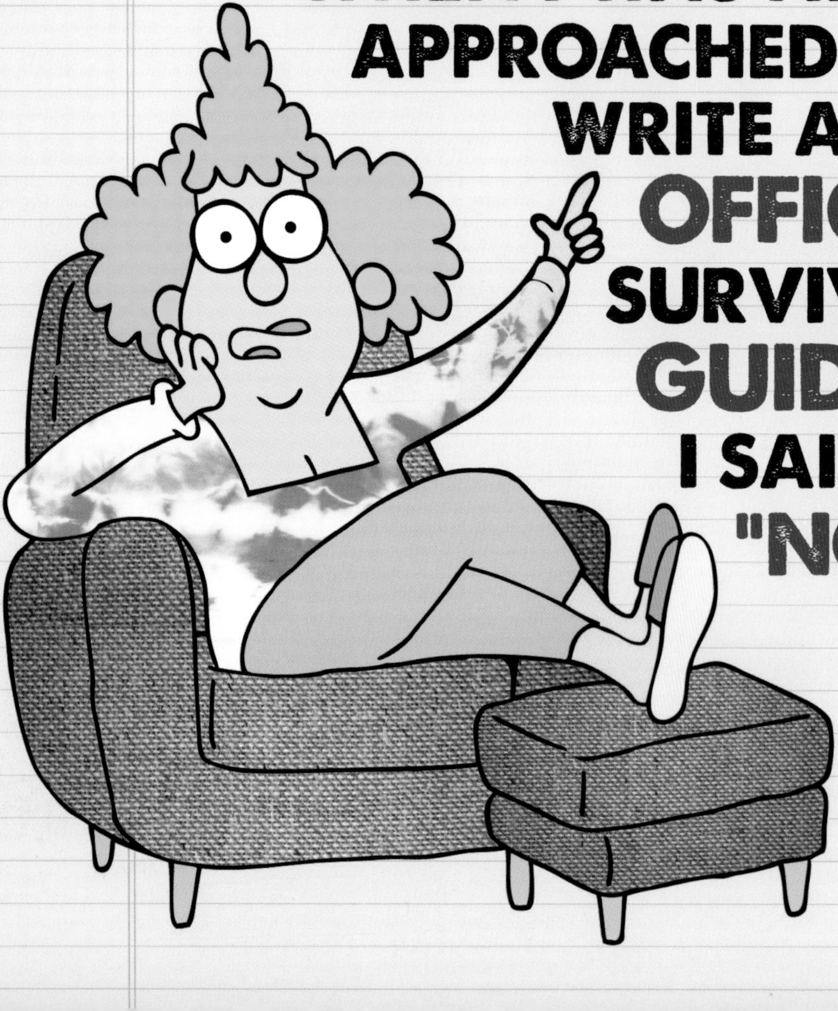

This came as a shock to a lot of people as 50% of my office capers are now accepted police training methods, while the other 50% form the backbone of every corporate video on how not to act at work.

My problem was that I didn't want my readers to simply "Survive," I want them to "Thrive." So in order to do that, I demanded that the manual show exactly what an office can throw at you and, more importantly, how to throw it right back!

In my opinion, using polite conversation to rectify matters only leads to resentment and increased drinking at the desk, while holding back your opinion is like trapping a bear in a paper bag—sooner or later, you know it's going to let rip.

So enjoy my manual and learn to say what you see when you see it. It may be blunt and offensive, but that's my style and it works. So if you're the first person in the office they think of when a really tough job is flying around, following this manual will help you to become the last person they'll ever think of to do anything!

AUNTY ACID

X

Meeting at 9:30? I'm sorry I can't, that's when I look at pictures of cats on the Internet.

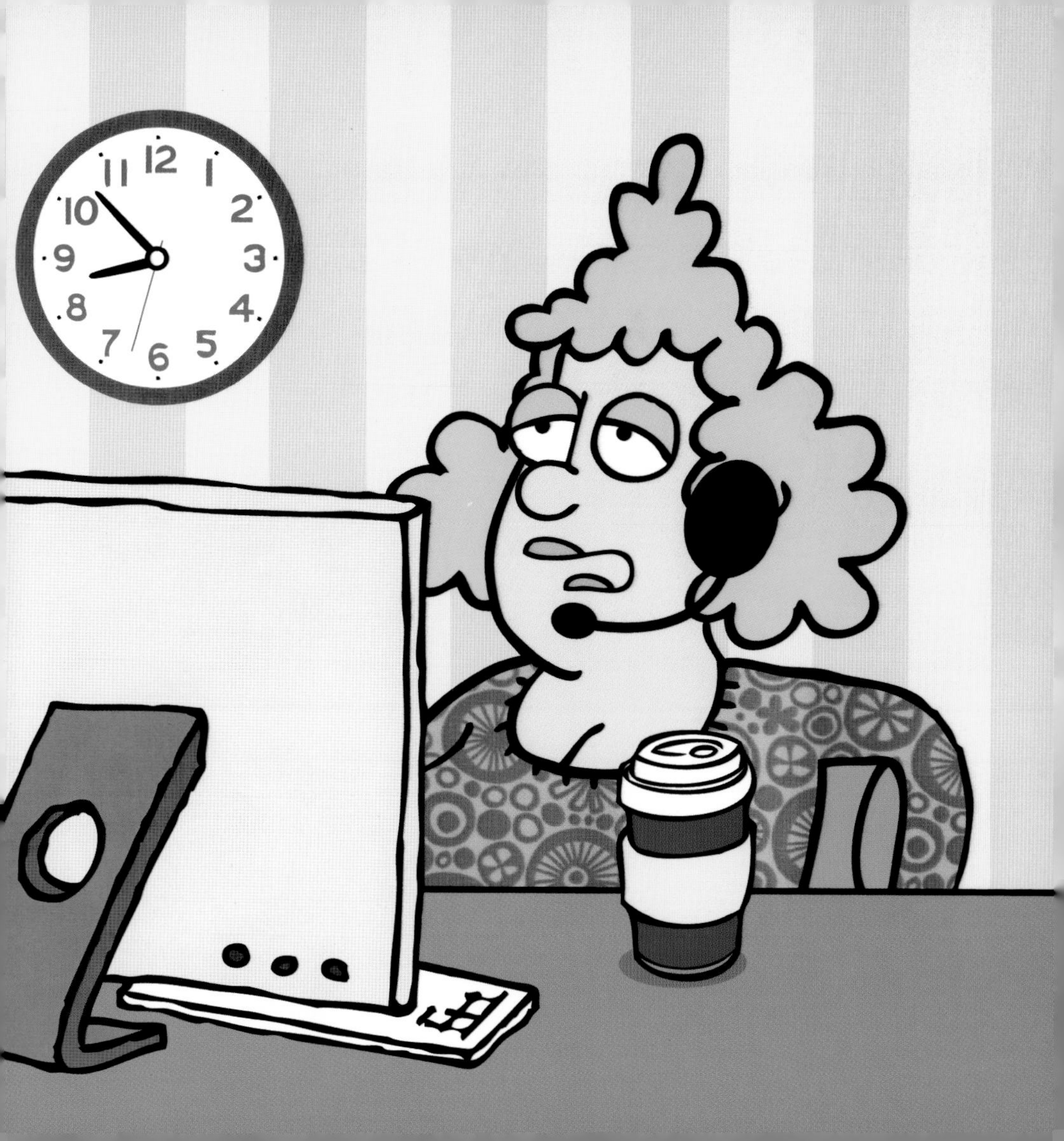

If you're quiet and you listen closely, you can hear the sound of Monday sharpening her claws.

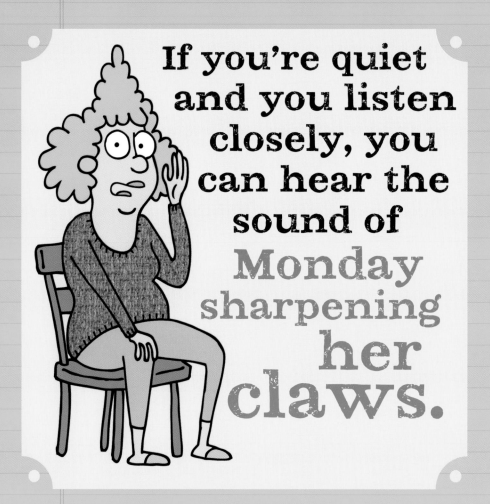

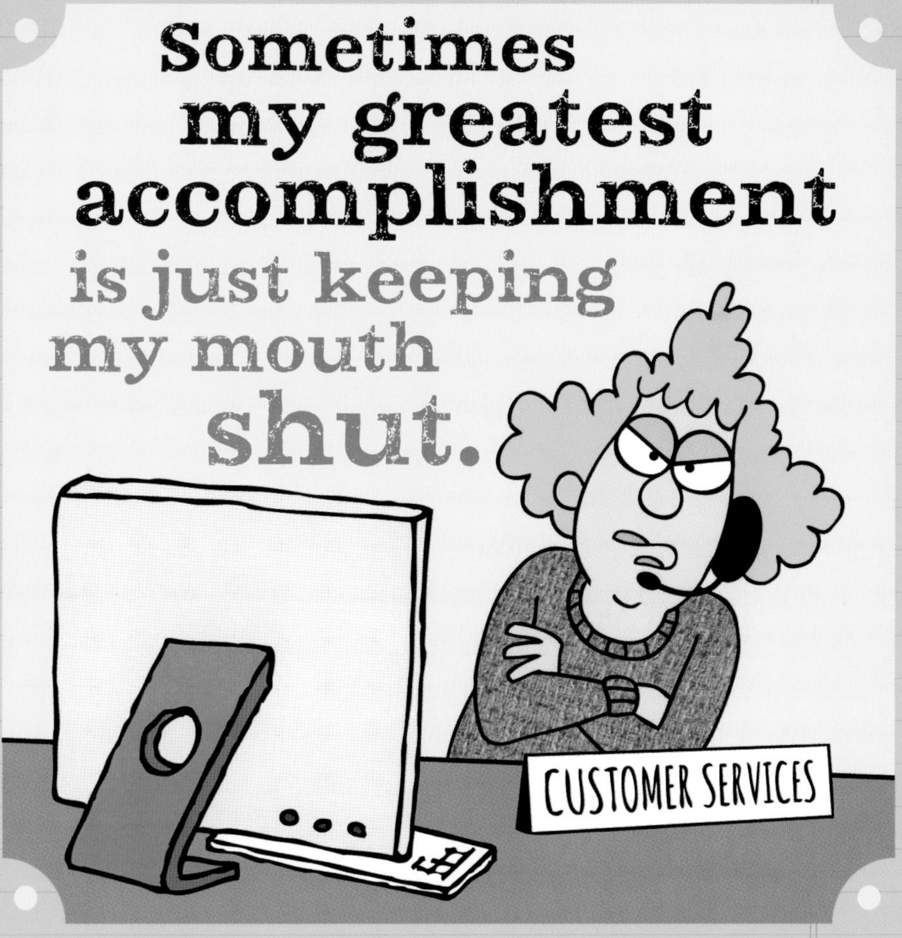
Sometimes
my greatest
accomplishment
is just keeping
my mouth
shut.
CUSTOMER SERVICES

I start each working day with a bucket list.

Item No. 1:

Fill it with coffee.

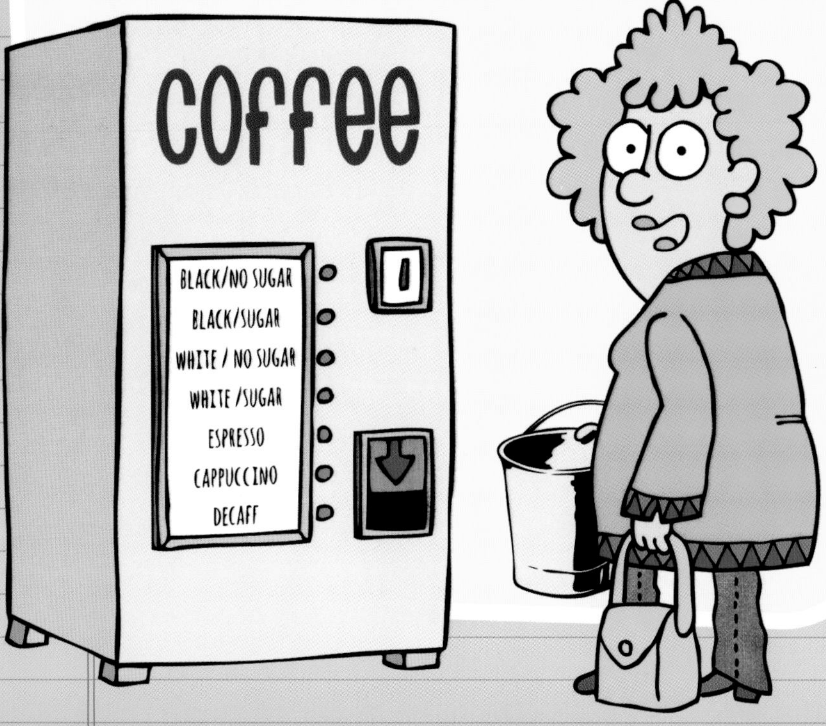
COFFEE
BLACK/NO SUGAR
BLACK/SUGAR
WHITE / NO SUGAR
WHITE /SUGAR
ESPRESSO
CAPPUCCINO
DECAFF

I admit it ain't the best-paid job I've ever had... and the hours are pretty long... and there ain't a lot of perks... but at least I've still got my dignity.

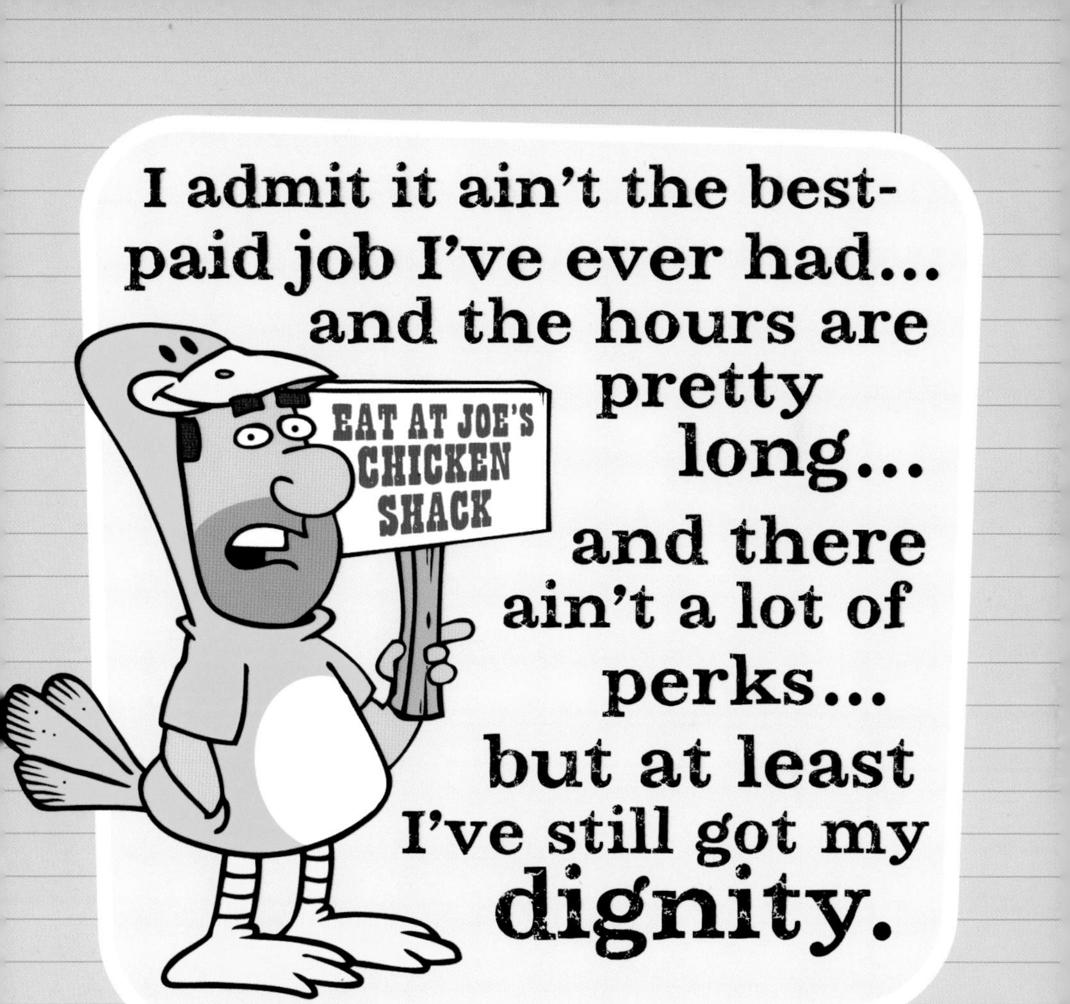
EAT AT JOE'S
CHICKEN
SHACK

It's weird how my salary exactly covers the cost of the alcohol I require to make going to work bearable.

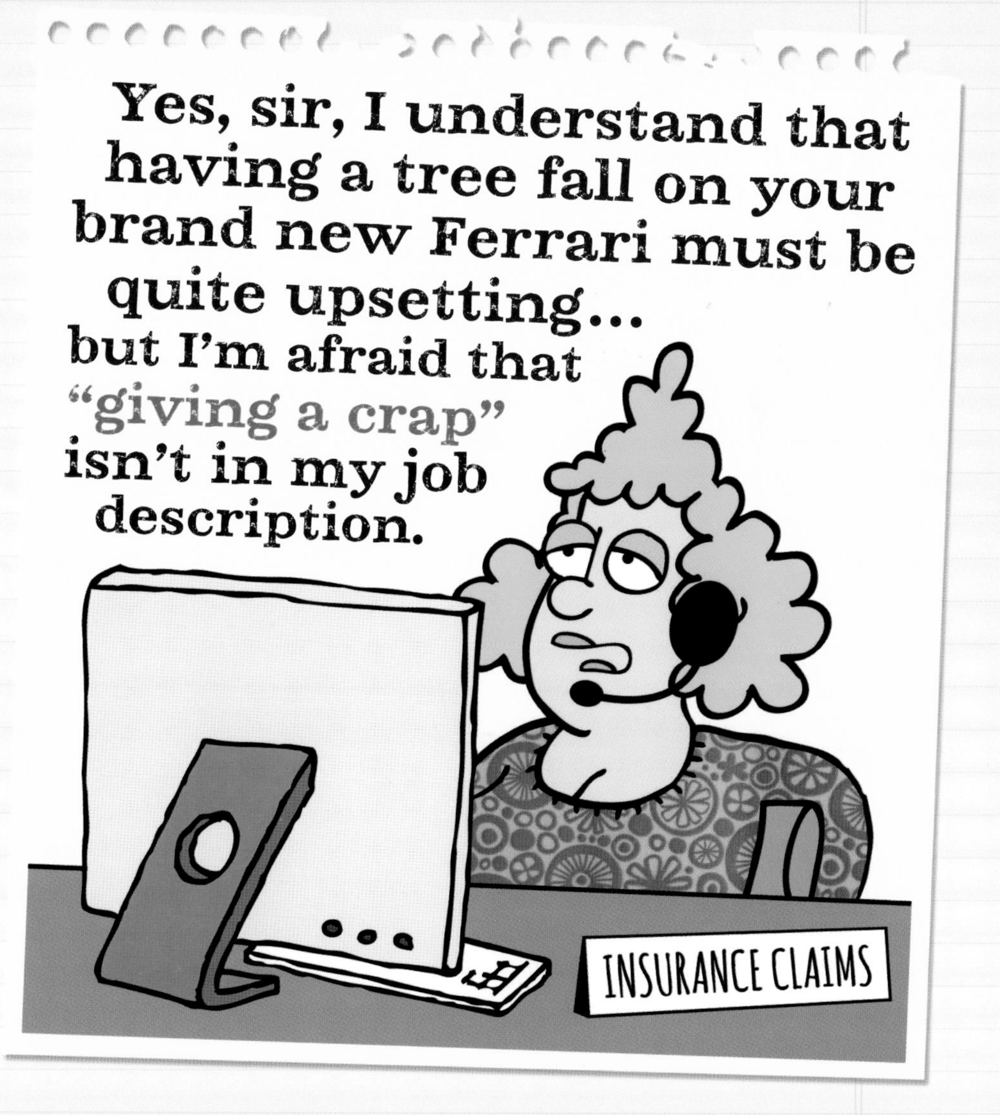
Yes, sir, I understand that having a tree fall on your brand new Ferrari must be quite upsetting... but I'm afraid that "giving a crap" isn't in my job description.
INSURANCE CLAIMS

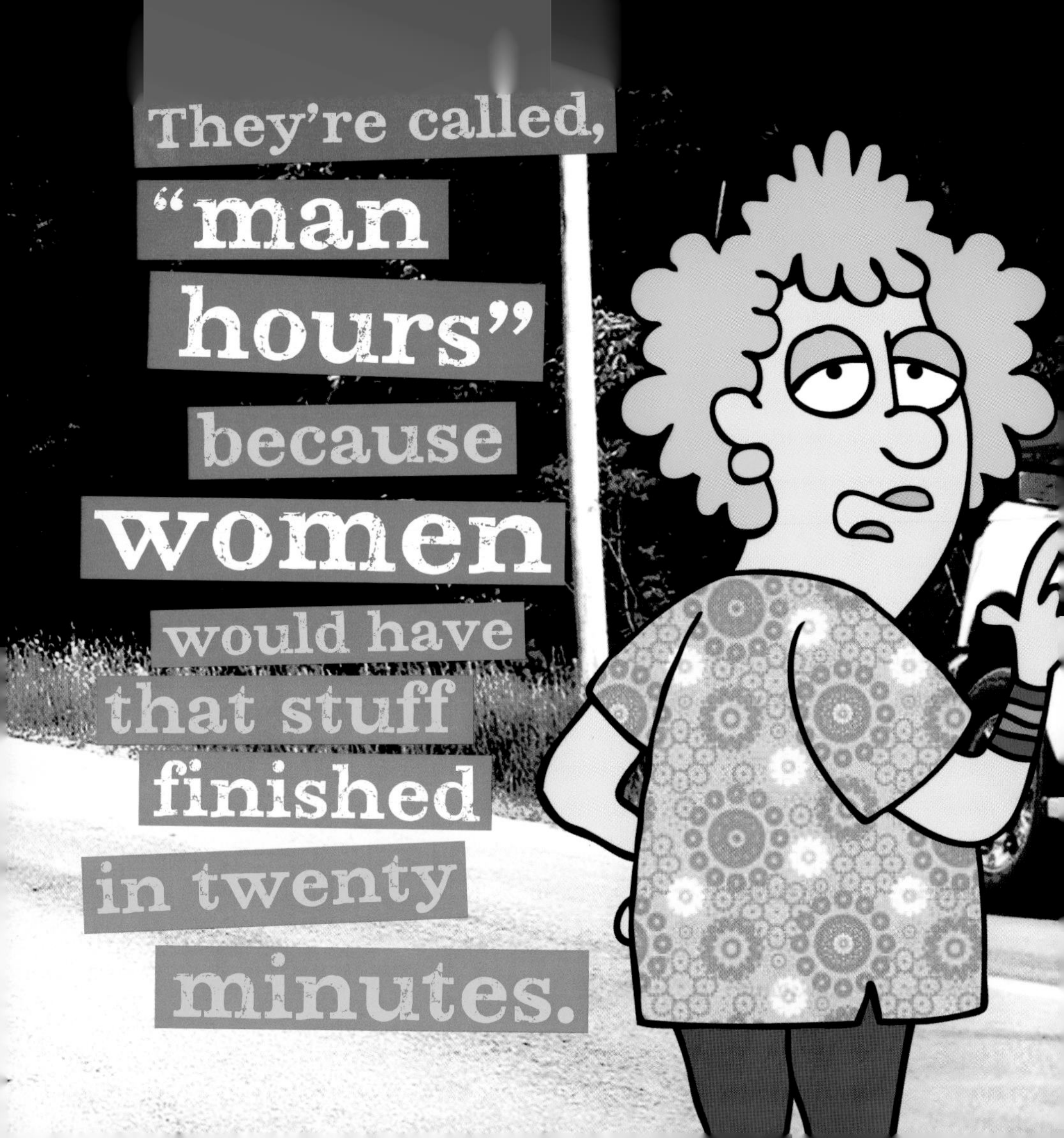
They're called,
"man
hours"
because
women
would have
that stuff
finished
in twenty
minutes.

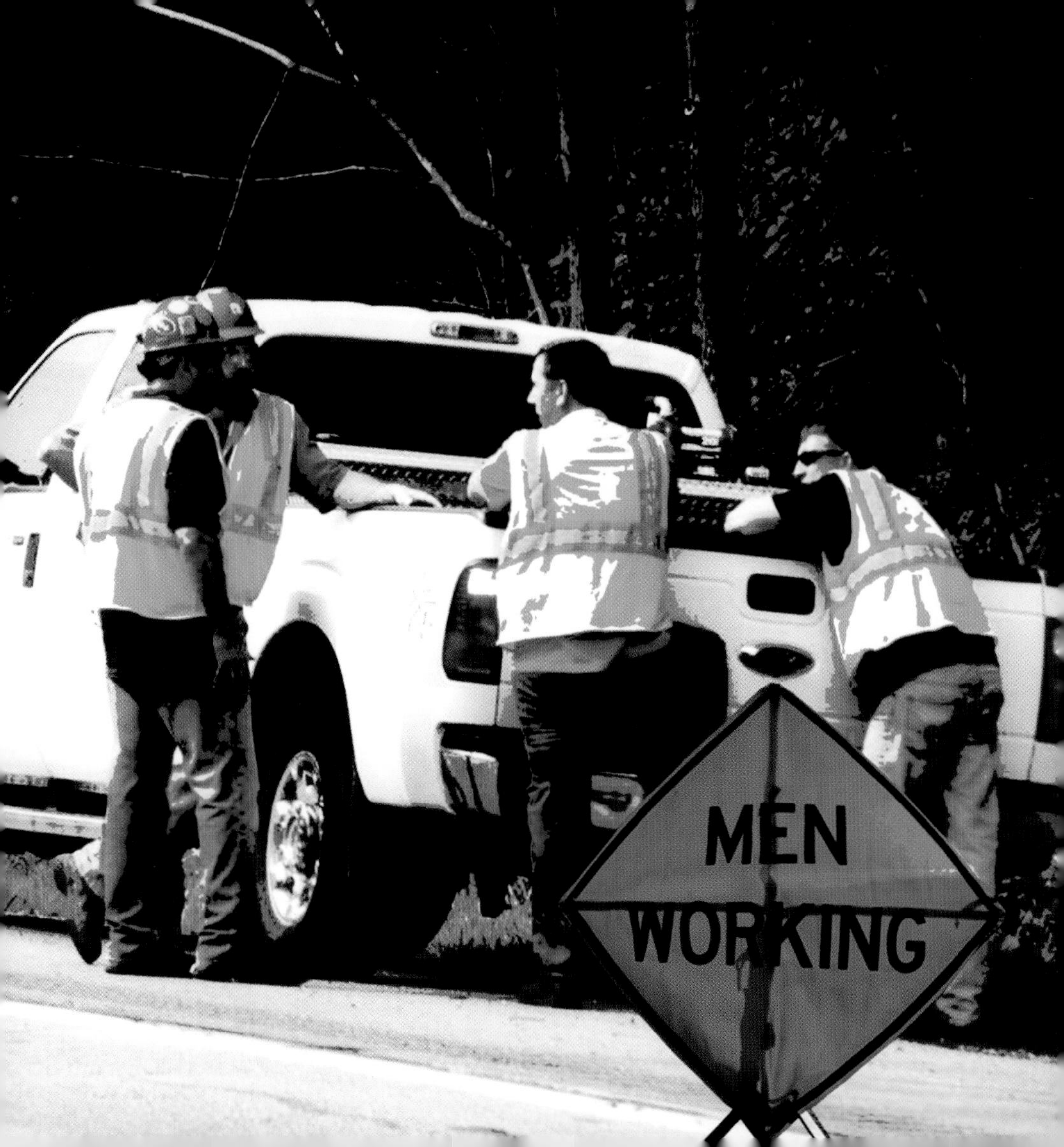
MEN
WORKING

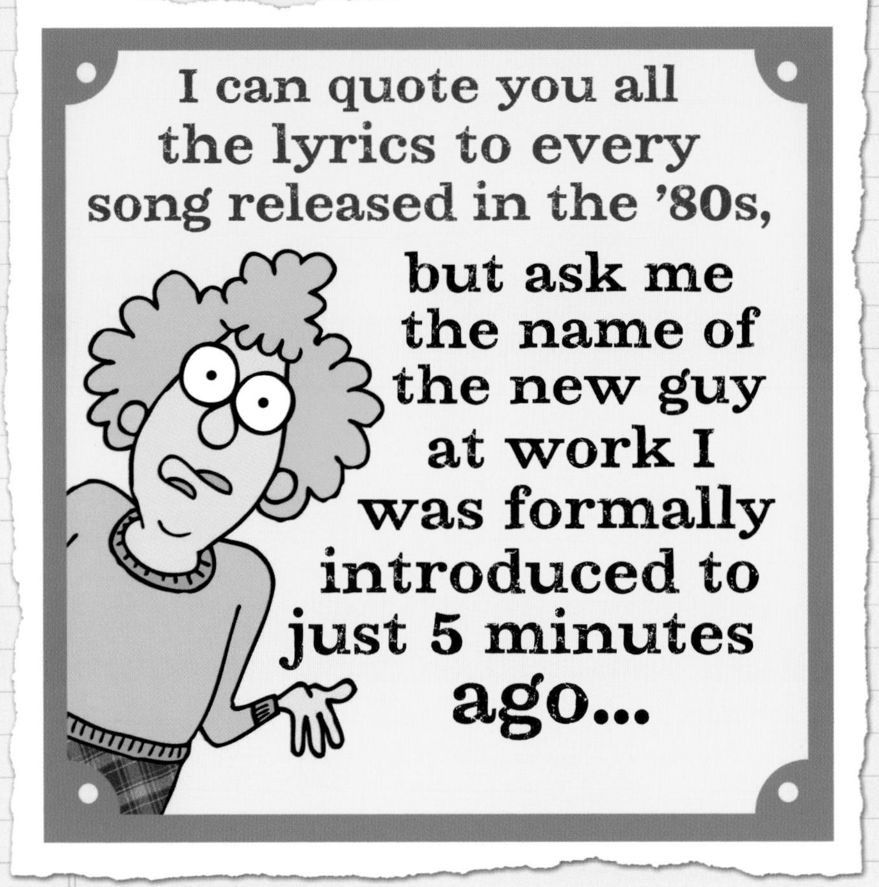
I can quote you all the lyrics to every song released in the '80s,
but ask me the name of the new guy at work I was formally introduced to just 5 minutes ago...

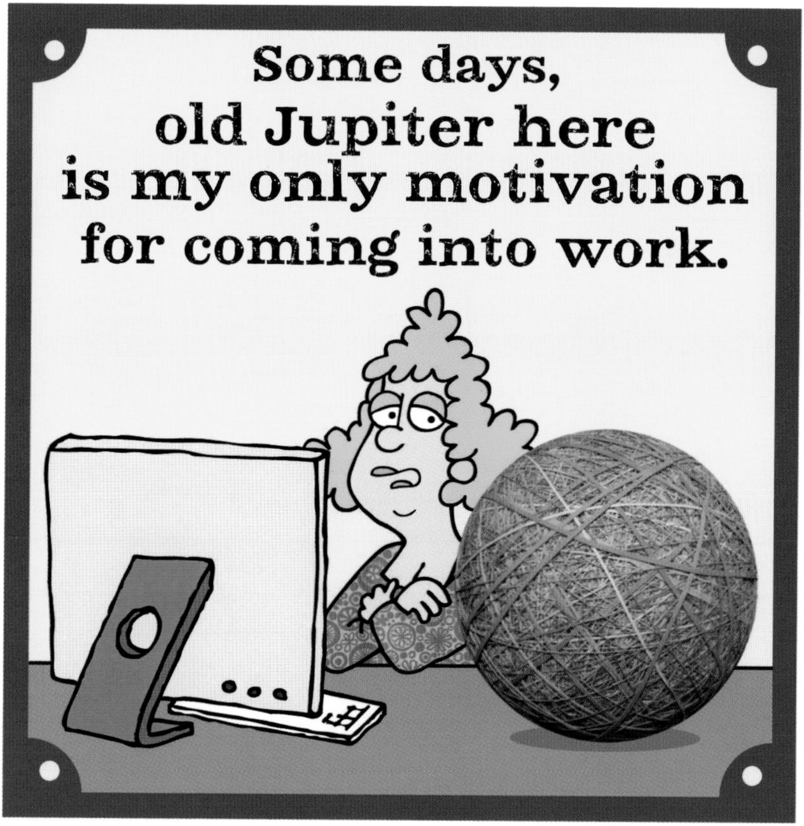
Some days,
old Jupiter here
is my only motivation
for coming into work.

It takes me, roughly, two-and-a-half hours to get my face ready for a quick run to the local store...

and you expect me to take a Skype call at 3 minutes' notice?

Dream on, Buster!

I always spend 20 minutes exercising before I set off to work each morning.

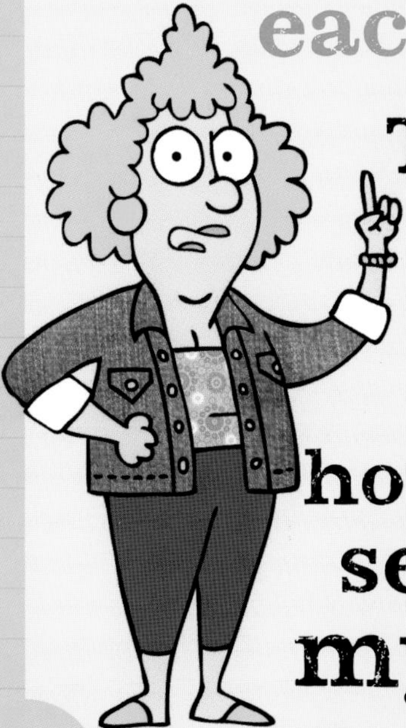

That's usually how long it takes to run around the house, frantically searching for my car keys.

I thought I'd found my groove...

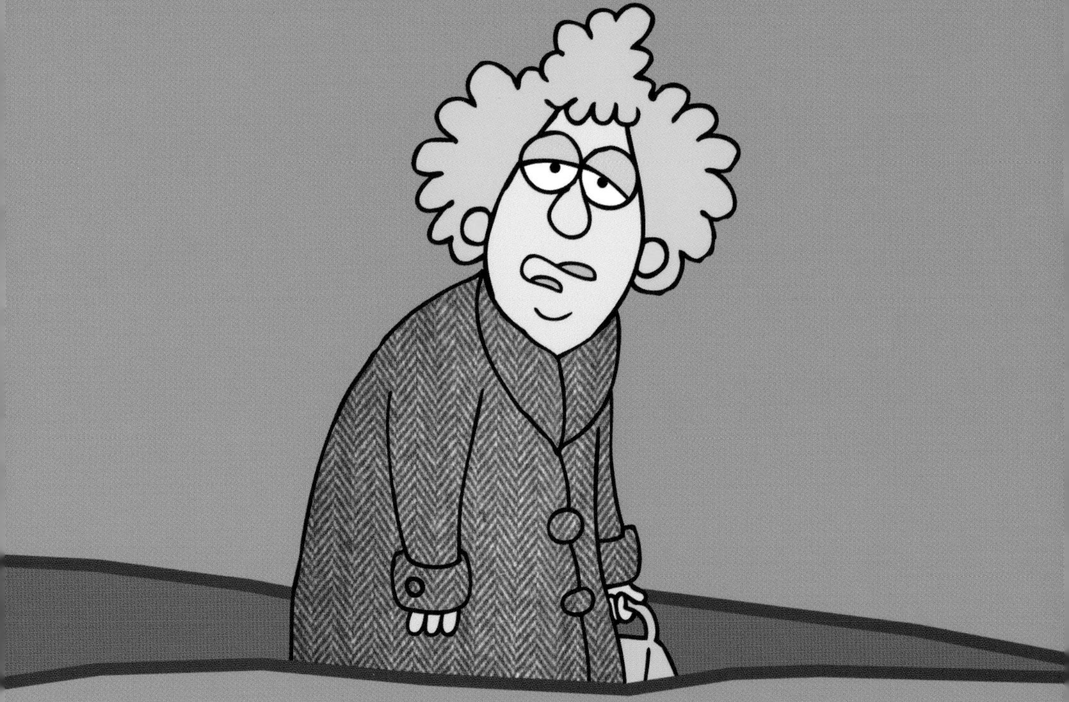

...turns out
it's a rut.

Don't you just hate it when you spend the entire night having bad dreams about going to work, then wake up and have to go to work?

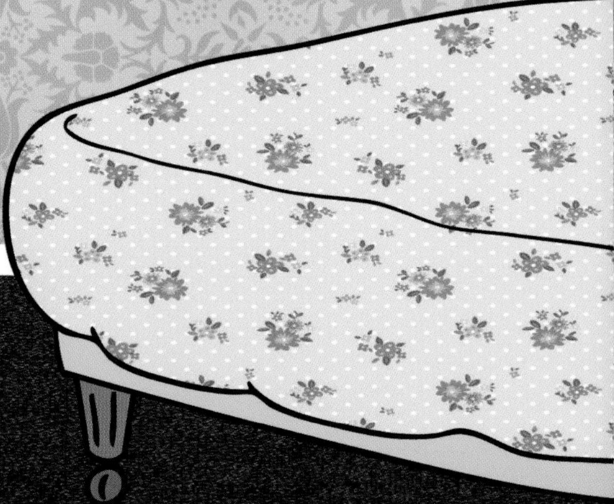

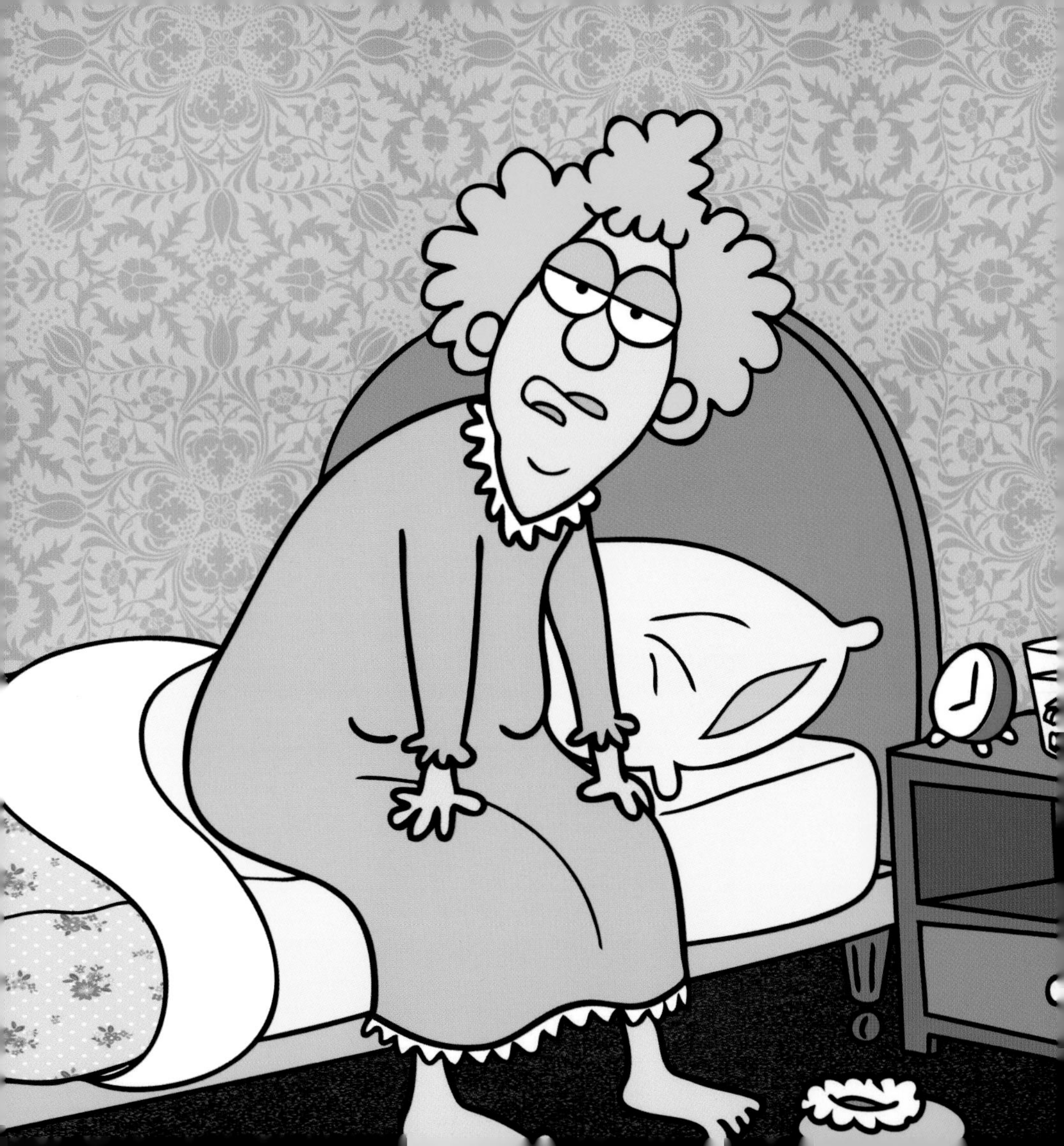

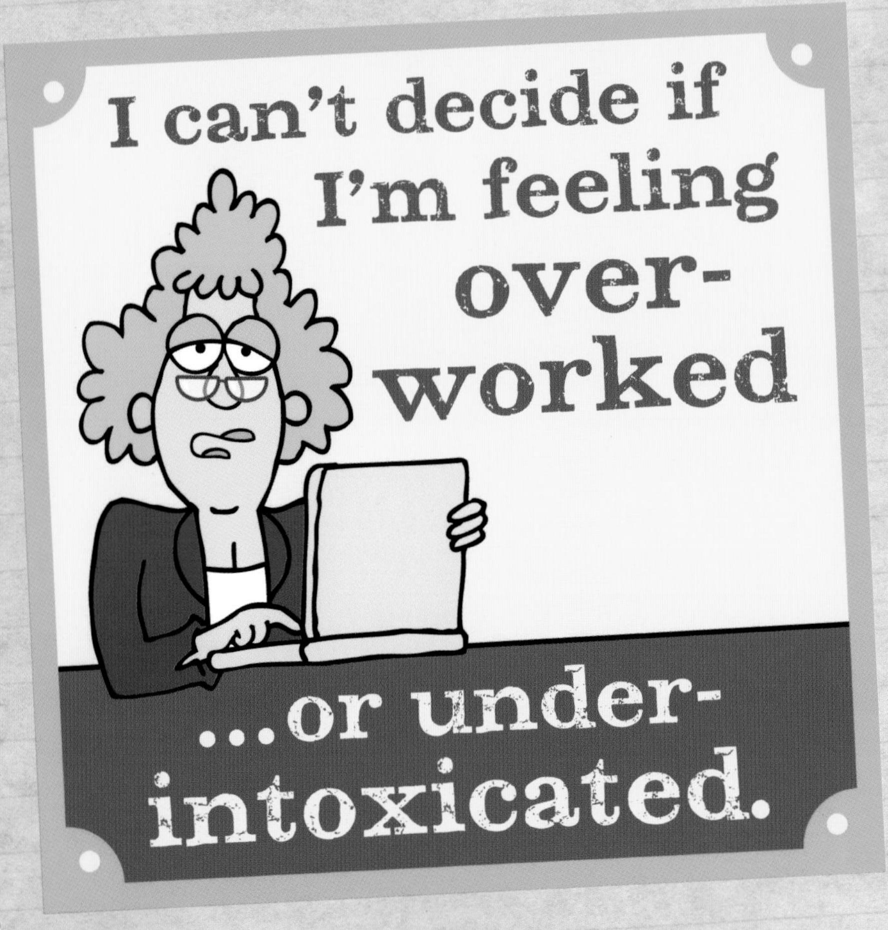
I can't decide if I'm feeling over-worked
...or under-intoxicated.

I got an email from work asking me if I'd like to sign up for a "Team Bonding Weekend."

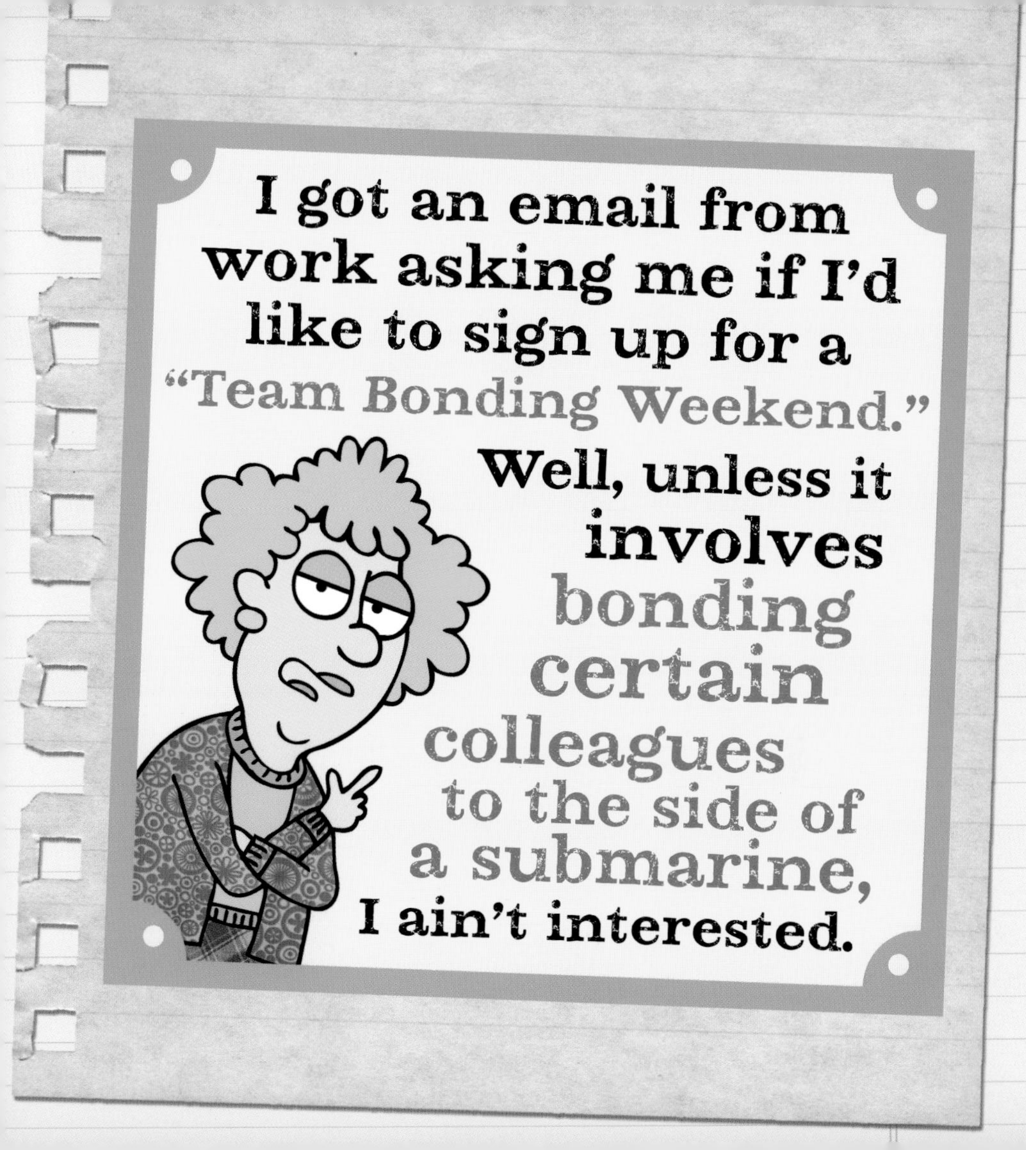

Well, unless it involves bonding certain colleagues to the side of a submarine, I ain't interested.

My first job was in the army... until I got my marching orders.

Then I tried my hand at being a postman...but soon got the sack.

After that I worked in a lingerie store for a while...before I was given a pink slip.

So I've just started a new job as a human cannonball ...although I've got an awful feeling I'm going to get fired tomorrow.

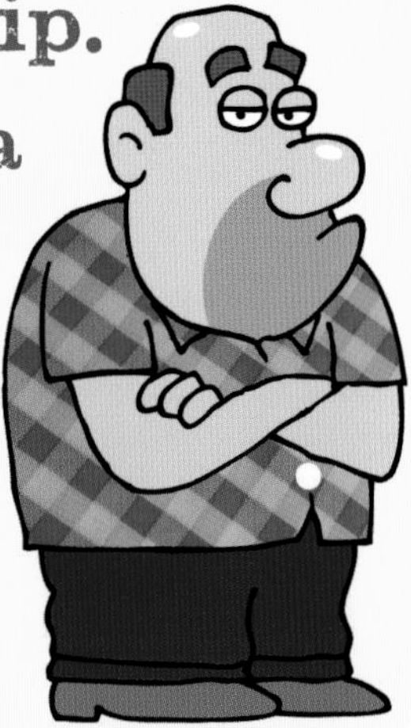

My boss asked me to write a report detailing all the things I enjoy about working for the company.

I got as far as "my chair swivels" and hit a dead end.

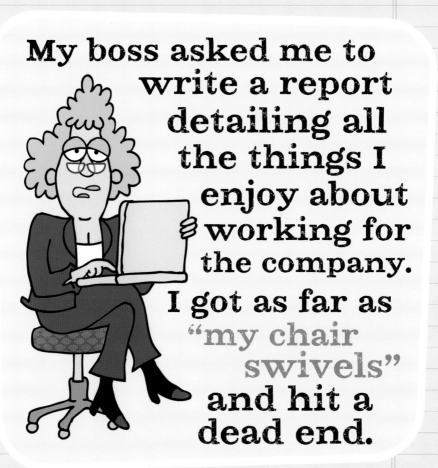

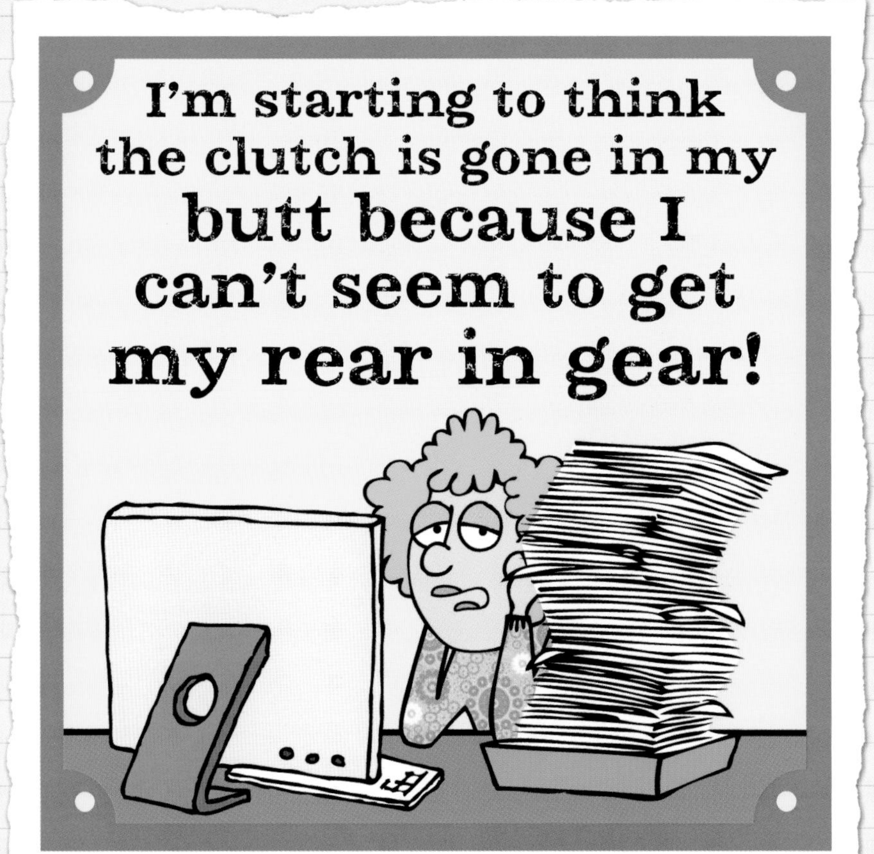
I'm starting to think the clutch is gone in my butt because I can't seem to get my rear in gear!

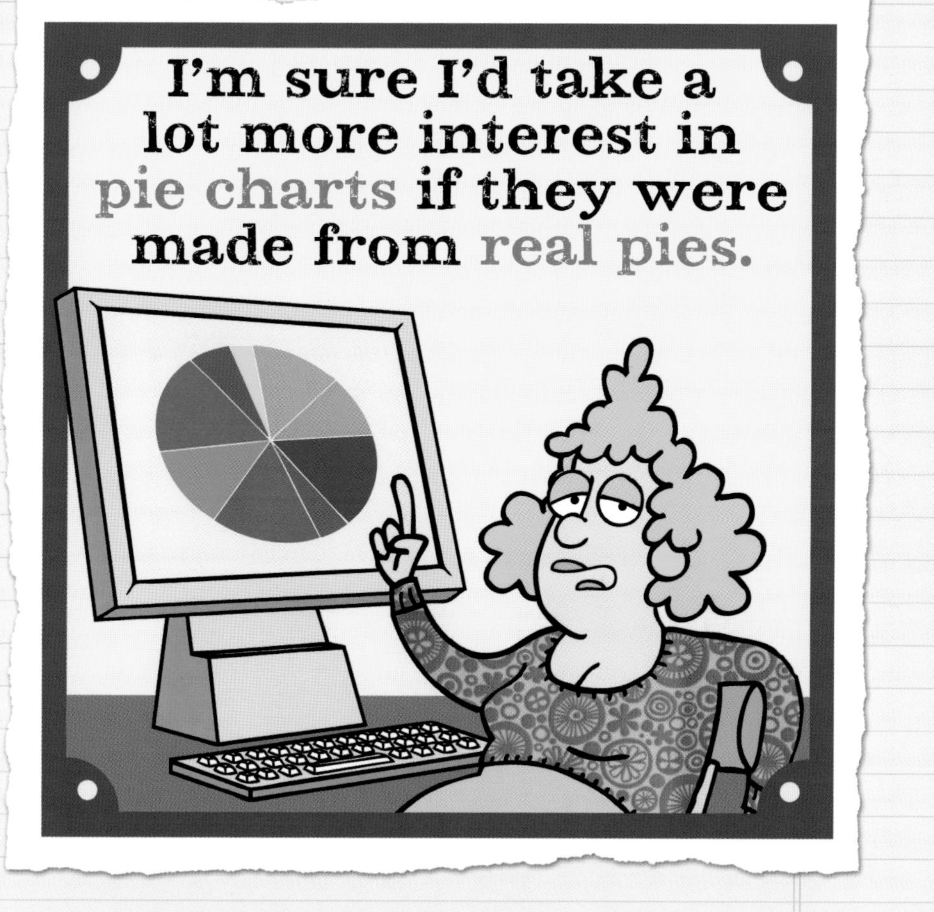
I'm sure I'd take a lot more interest in pie charts if they were made from real pies.

BRING COFFEE
AND A DONUT.
GENTLY PLACE THEM
ON MY DESK WITHOUT
SPEAKING OR MAKING
EYE CONTACT, THEN
BACK AWAY SLOWLY
...AND MAYBE WE CAN
GET THROUGH THIS
WITHOUT ANYONE
GETTING HURT.

Stealing stuff from work isn’t half as much fun when you’re self-employed.

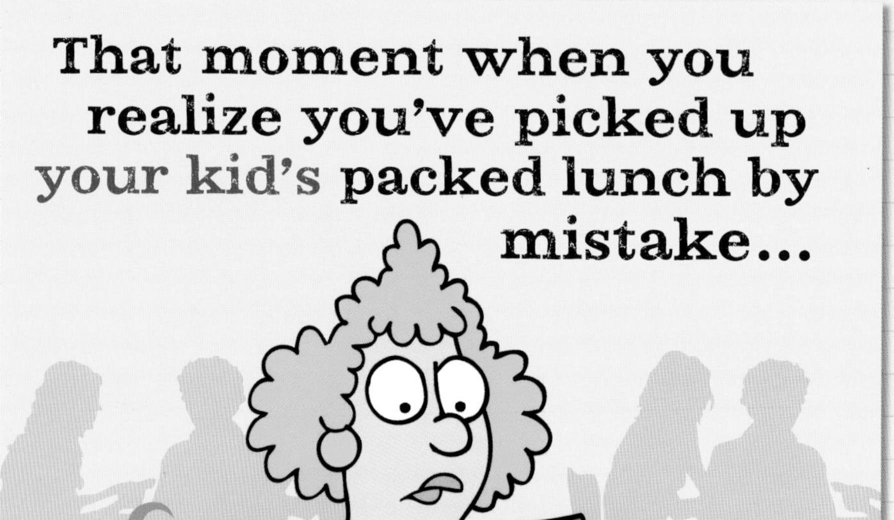
That moment when you realize you've picked up your kid's packed lunch by mistake...
Lunch
Milk
...and he's just discovered your quarter bottle of vodka.

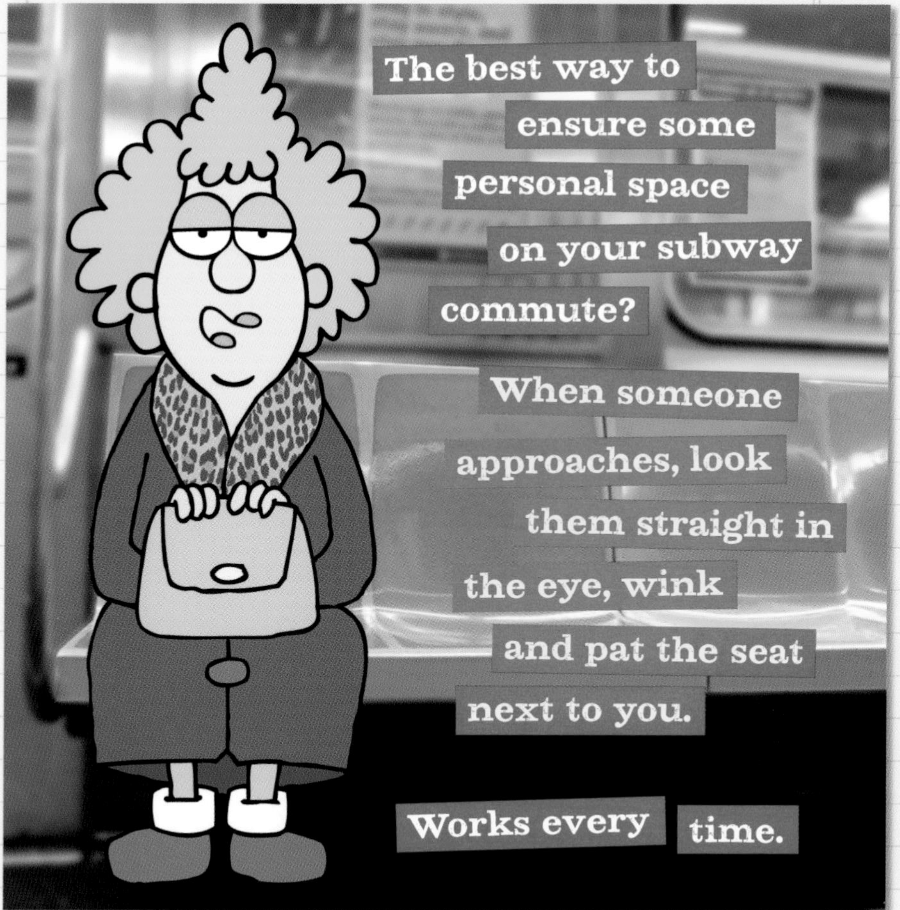
The best way to
ensure some
personal space
on your subway
commute?
When someone
approaches, look
them straight in
the eye, wink
and pat the seat
next to you.
Works every time.

I find the first five days after the weekend are the hardest.

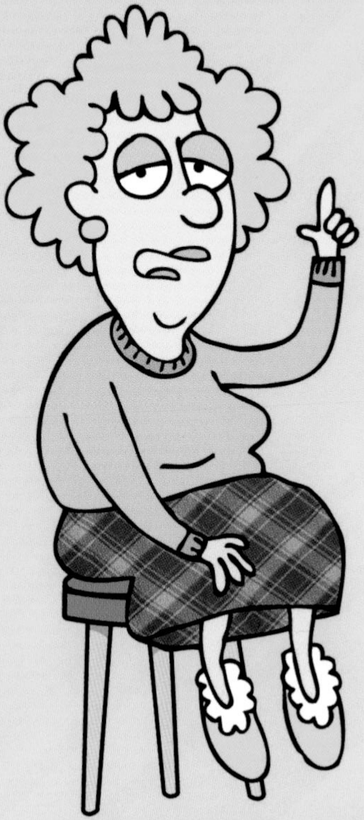

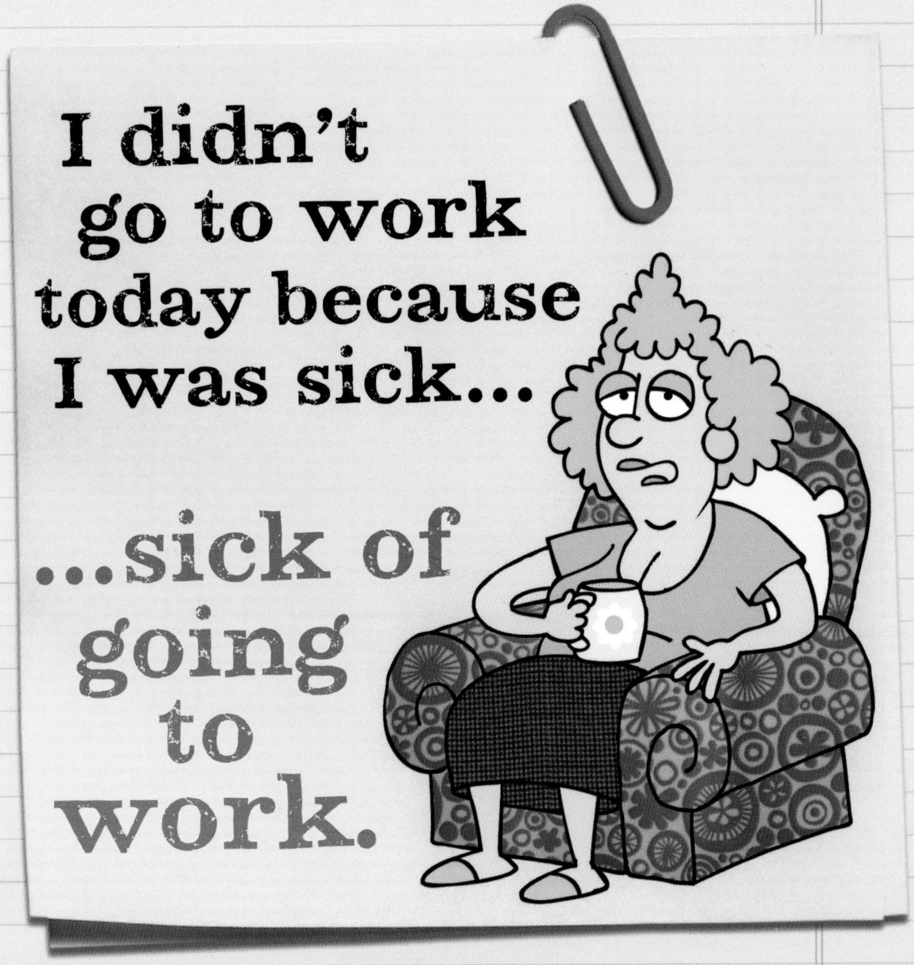
I didn't go to work today because I was sick...
...sick of going to work.

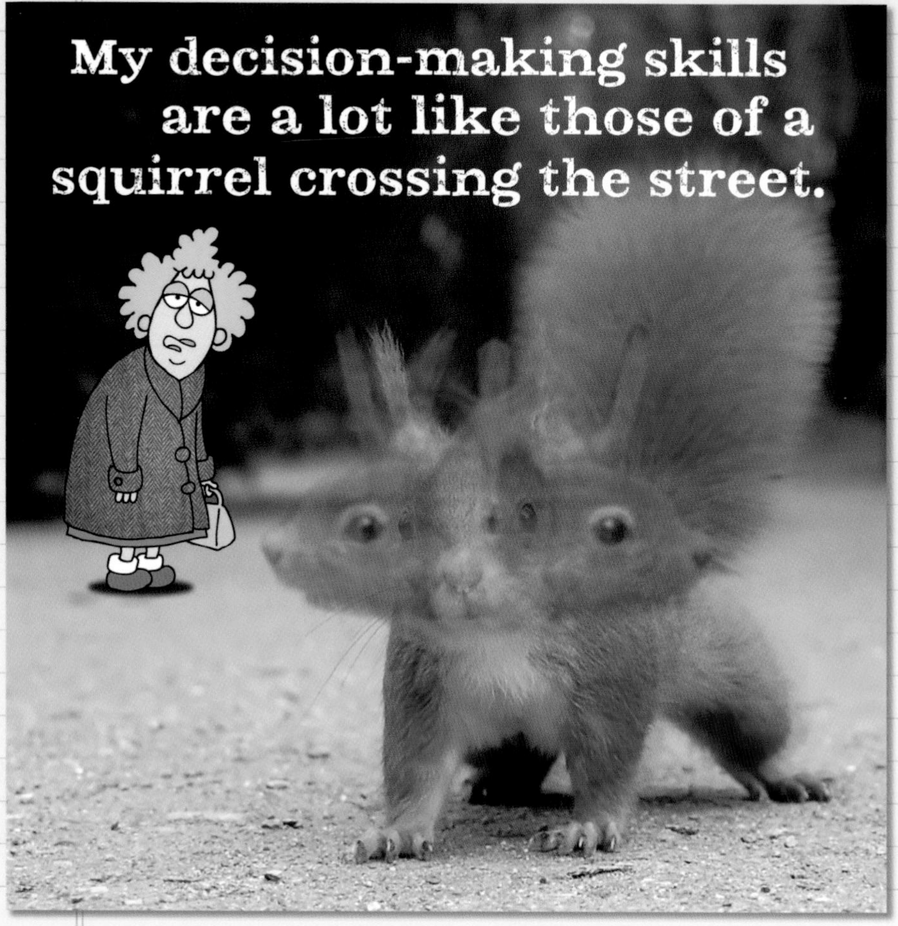
My decision-making skills are a lot like those of a squirrel crossing the street.

Of course I give 100% at work.

Usually 22% Monday through Thursday and 12% on Friday.

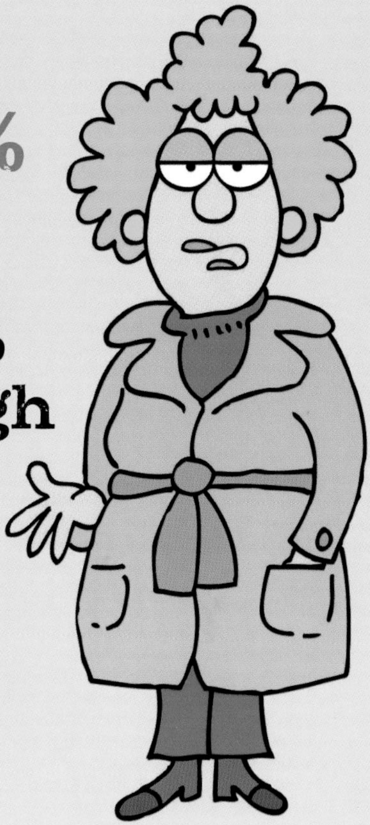

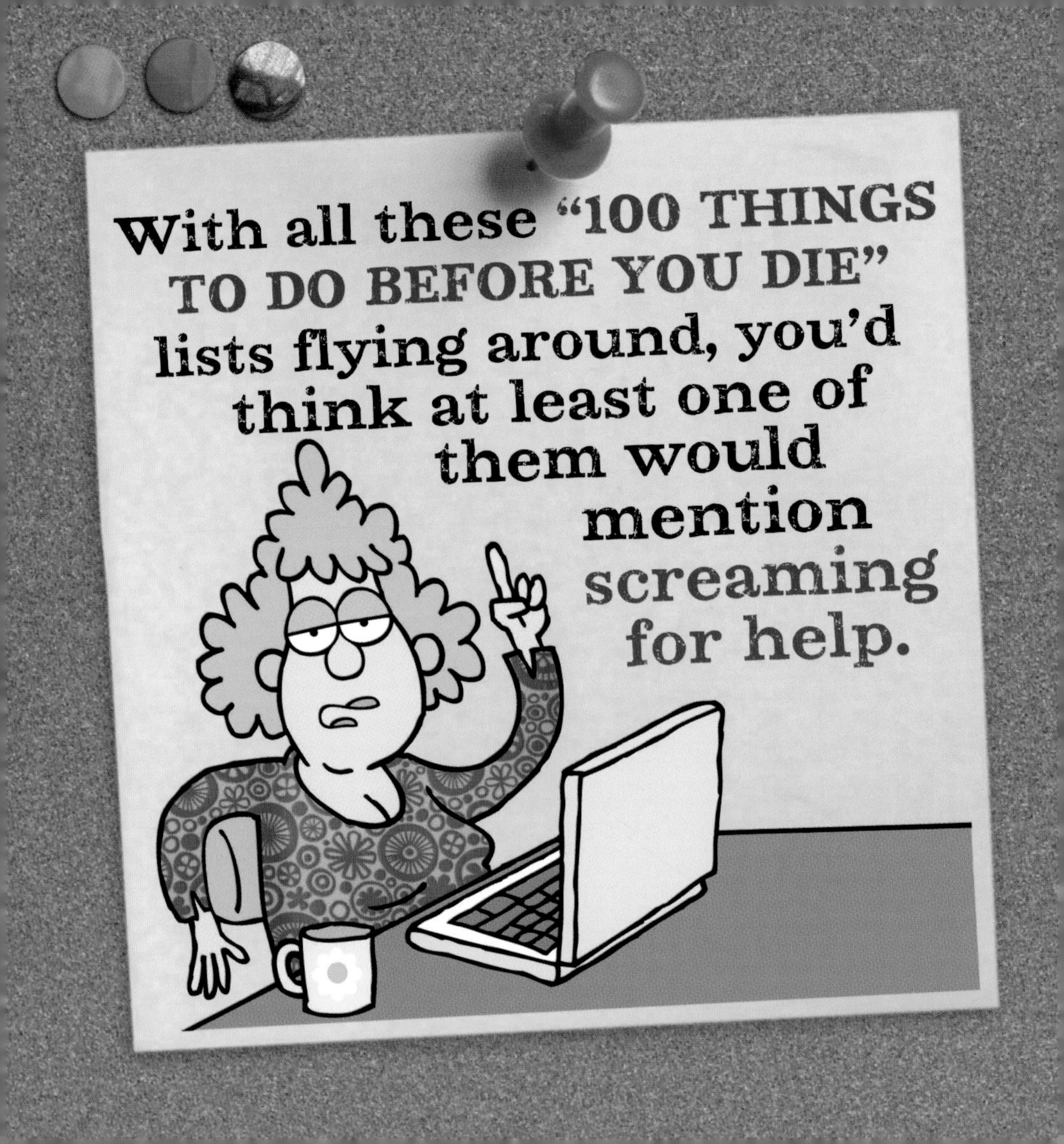
With all these "100 THINGS TO DO BEFORE YOU DIE" lists flying around, you'd think at least one of them would mention screaming for help.

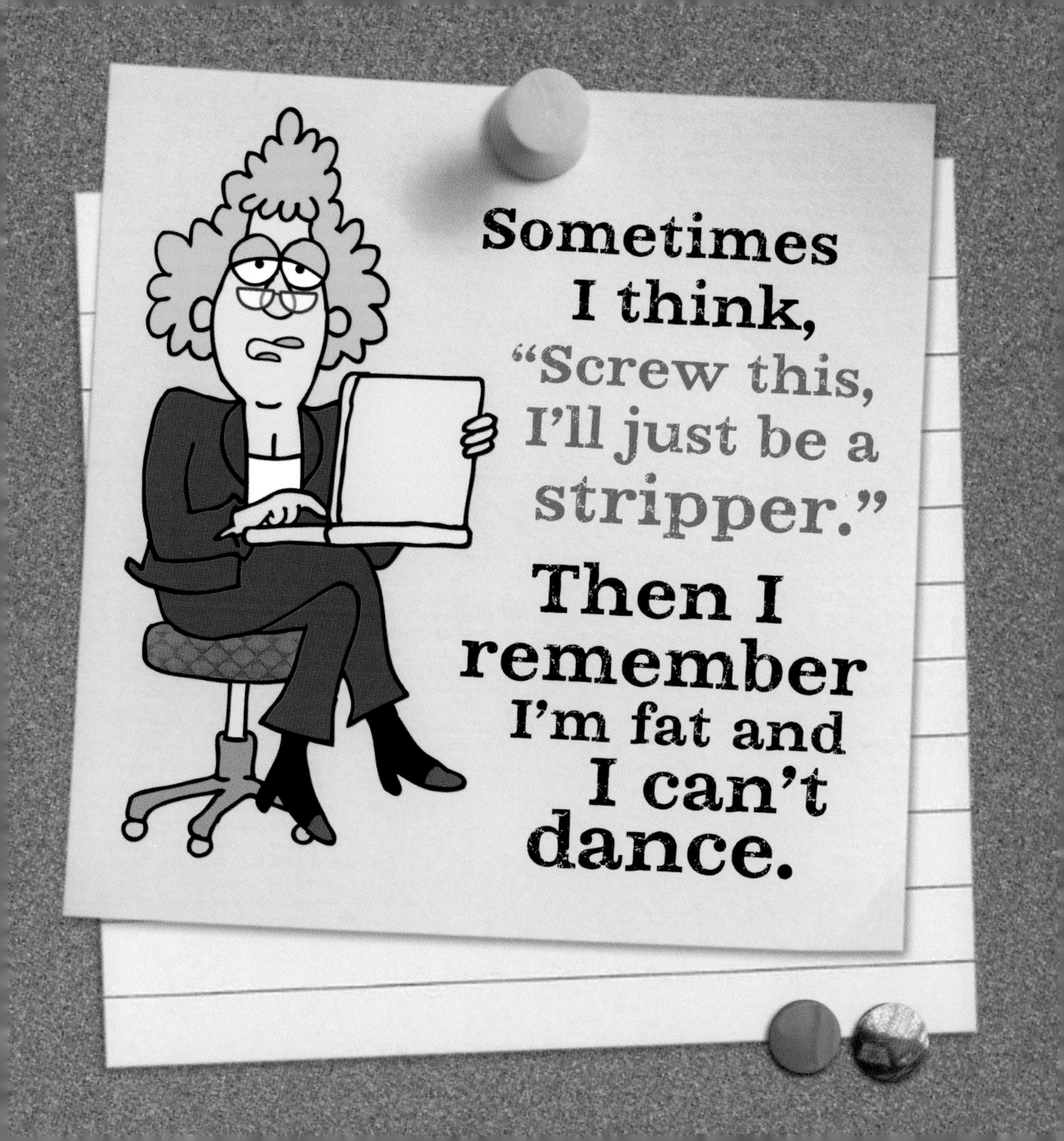

Sometimes I think, "Screw this, I'll just be a stripper." Then I remember I'm fat and I can't dance.

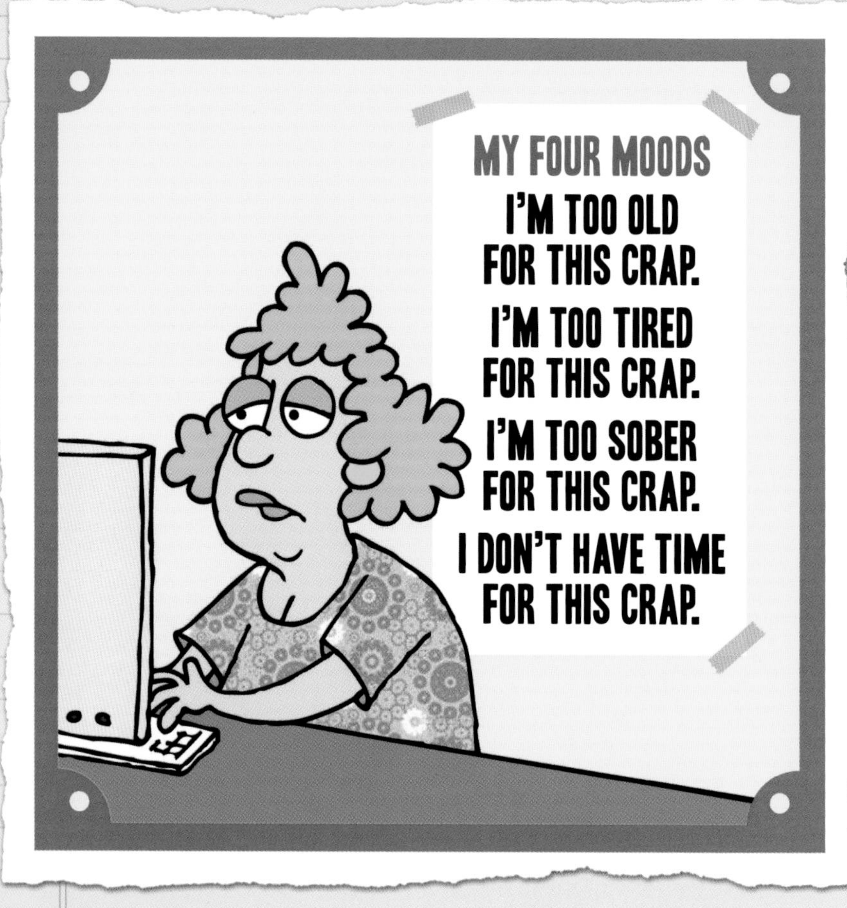
MY FOUR MOODS
I'M TOO OLD
FOR THIS CRAP.
I'M TOO TIRED
FOR THIS CRAP.
I'M TOO SOBER
FOR THIS CRAP.
I DON'T HAVE TIME
FOR THIS CRAP.

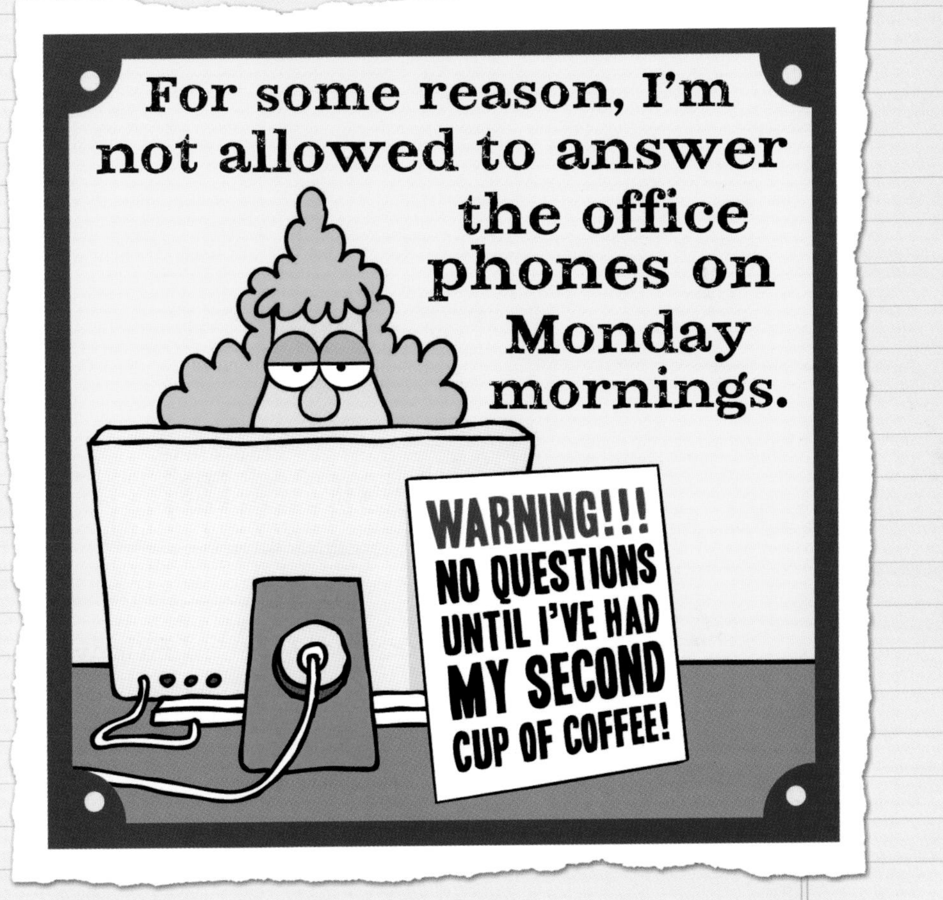
For some reason, I'm not allowed to answer the office phones on Monday mornings.
WARNING!!!
NO QUESTIONS UNTIL I'VE HAD MY SECOND CUP OF COFFEE!

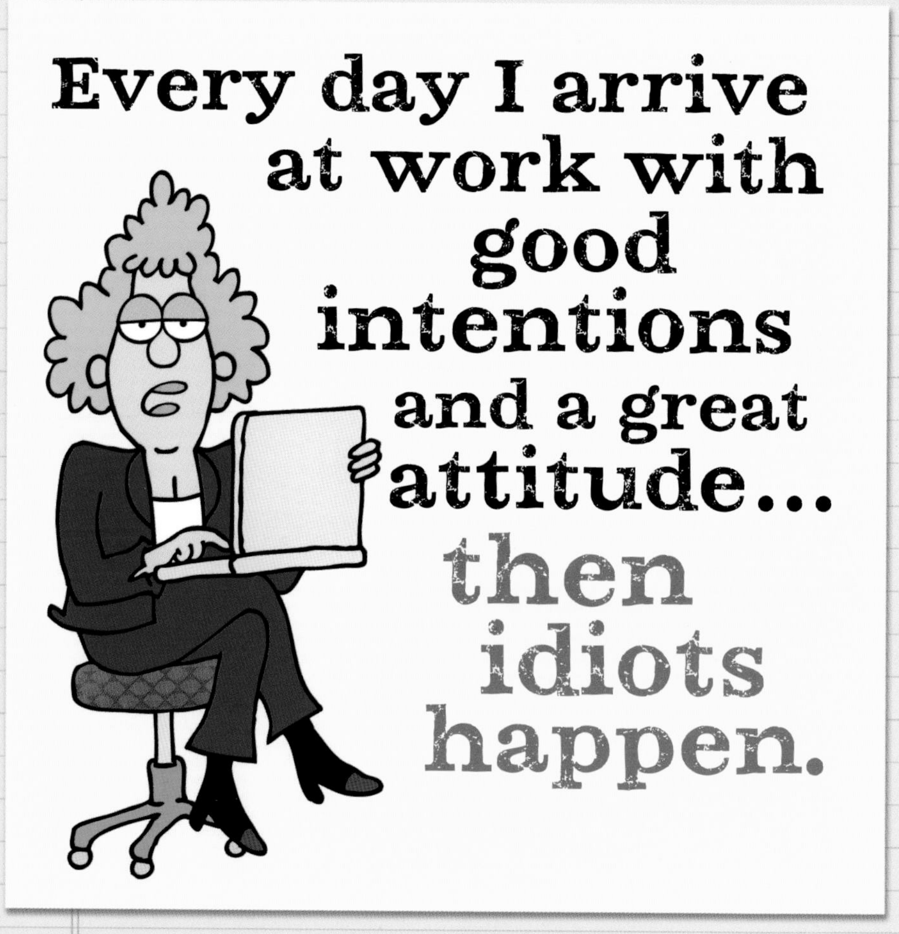
Every day I arrive at work with good intentions and a great attitude...
then idiots happen.

The boss's door is always open for me...because if he shuts it, I sneak off home early.
BOSS

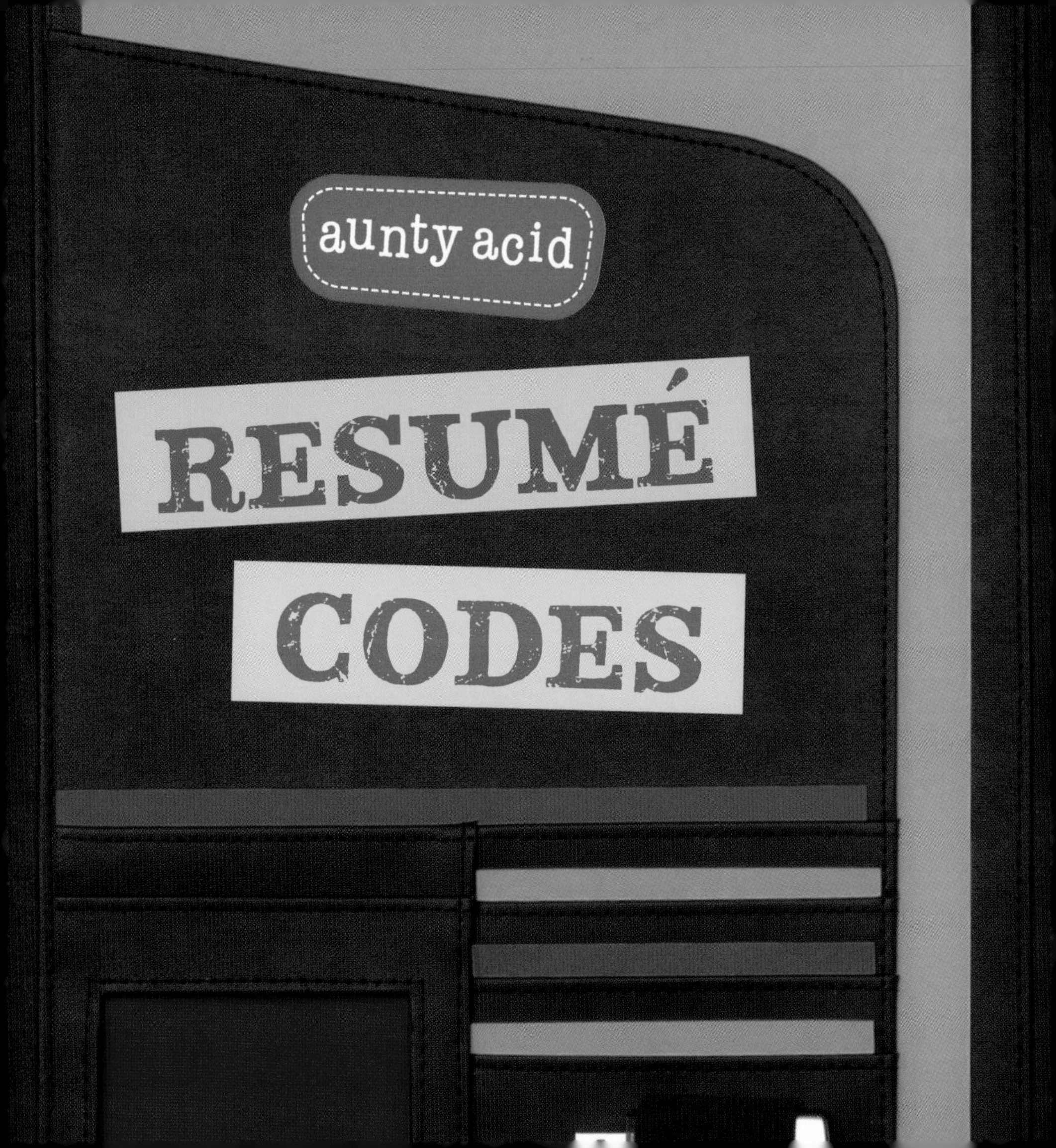
aunty acid
RESUMÉ
CODES

When it comes to hiring a new employee, please follow these simple codes:

Enthusiastic: Keen idiot

Team Player:
Likes to have others to blame

Experienced:
Had ten different jobs in the last month

Mature approach: Likes to nap during shift

Works great on their own:
Doesn't like witnesses

Conscientious:
Squeals on fellow workers

Good time manager: Sleeps in their car

Dependable:
Guaranteed to be found on the scene of all workplace accidents

---

Industrious: Makes small jobs look huge

COP CODES

734: Having a nap

746: Donut sugar on uniform

890: Using pepper spray on pizza

902: Trapped in own handcuffs

912: Suddenly woken by speeding car

933: Gone home for a coffee

944: Fully armed while shopping

949: Need bomb disposal truck to move sister-in-law's freezer

---

954: Need location of nearest drive-through burger joint

988: SWAT team needed to open beer keg

PLUMBER CODES

Big job:
Your home will be full of people doing nothing

Tricky:
Has no idea what the problem is

Delicate Job: Will be working with a hangover

Special parts needed:
Lots of over-priced plastic pipes on site

Estimated cost: Half the price it will actually be

Labor intensive: Workers won't be speaking English

Special parts:
Will be using whatever's left on the truck

Messy job: Your home will be wrecked

Start date: Your check cleared

Completion date: Your bank account is empty

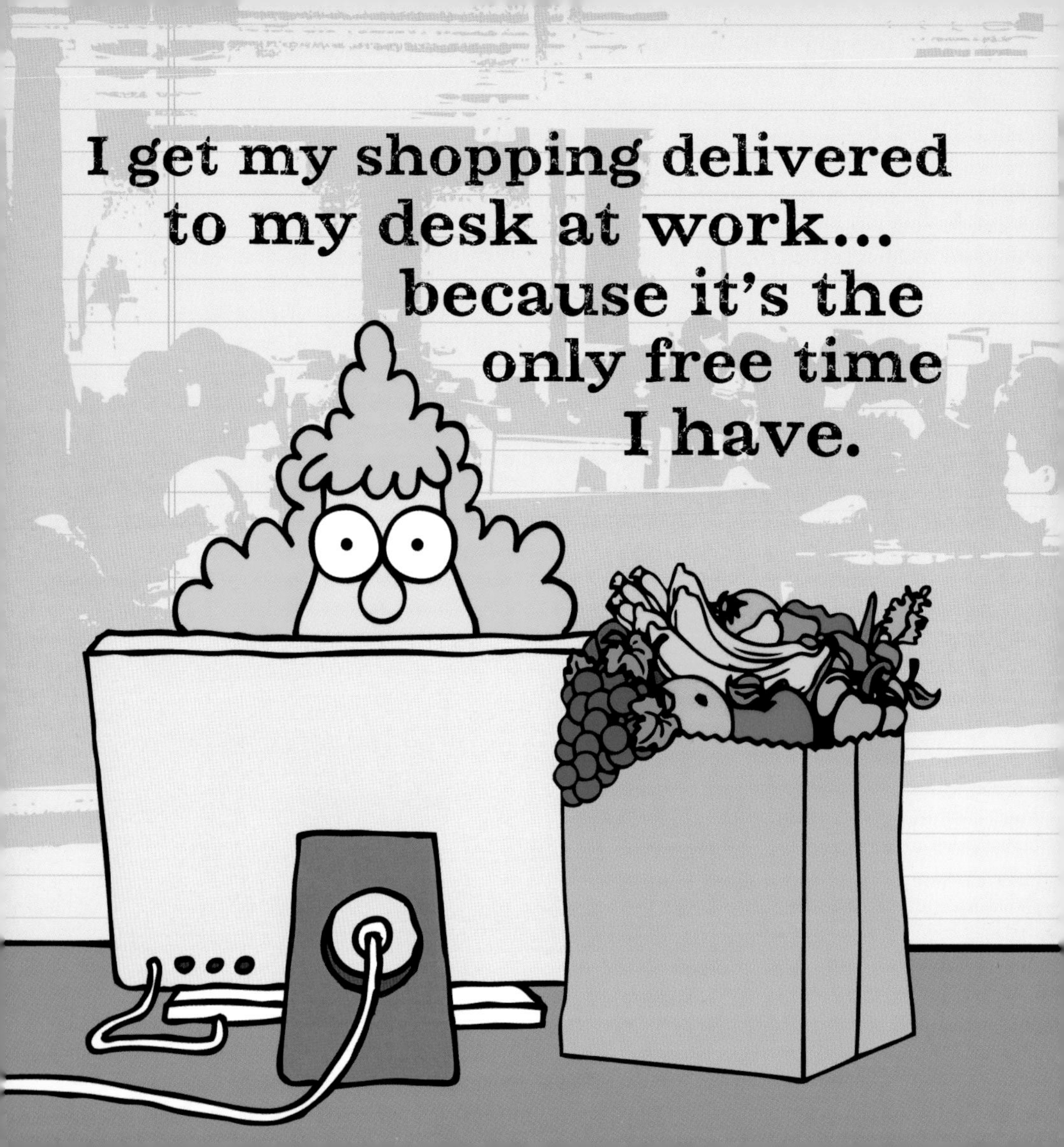
I get my shopping delivered to my desk at work... because it's the only free time I have.

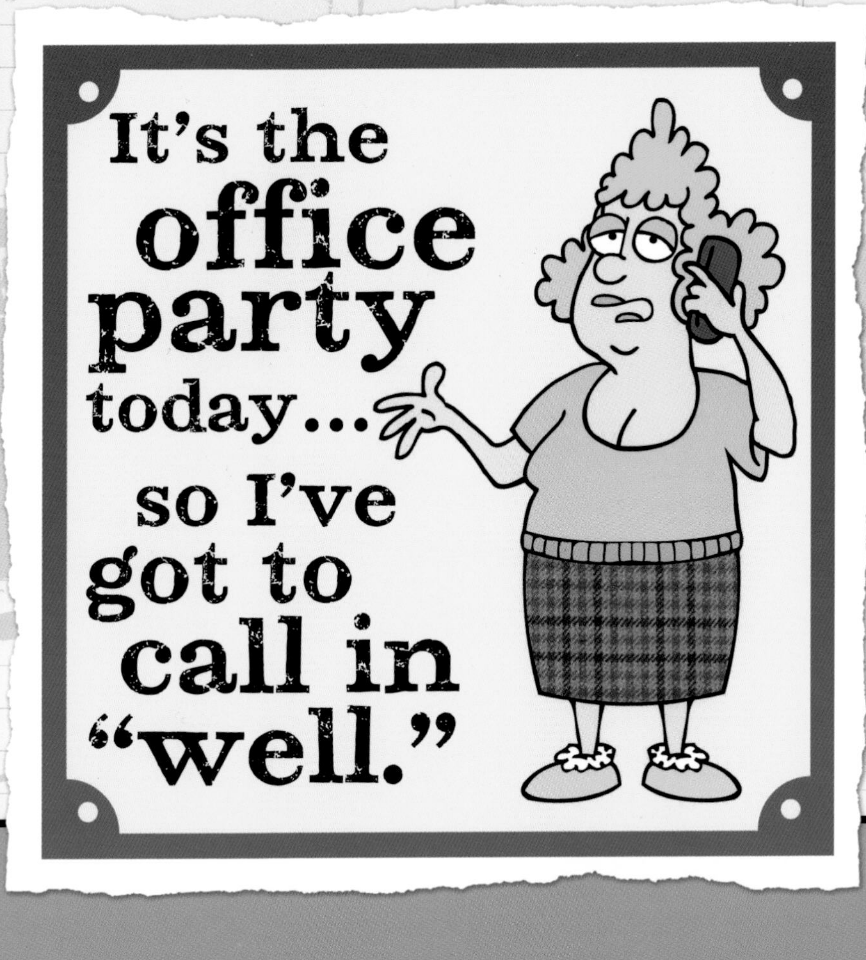
It's the
office
party
today...
so I've
got to
call in
"well."

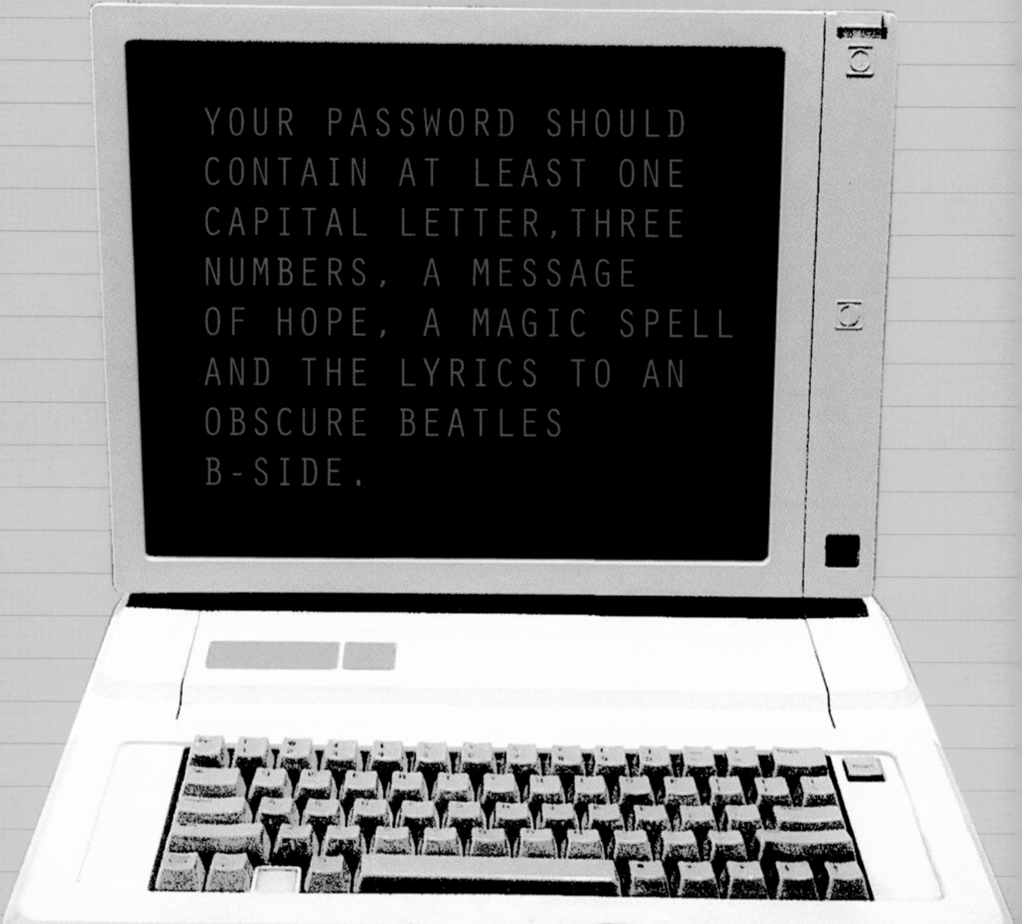
YOUR PASSWORD SHOULD
CONTAIN AT LEAST ONE
CAPITAL LETTER,THREE
NUMBERS, A MESSAGE
OF HOPE, A MAGIC SPELL
AND THE LYRICS TO AN
OBSCURE BEATLES
B-SIDE.

My boss asked me to see things from his point of view.

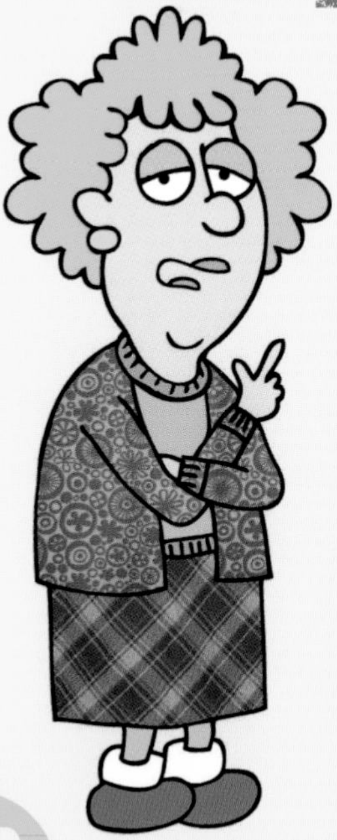

I replied, "I would if only I could fit my head up my butt."

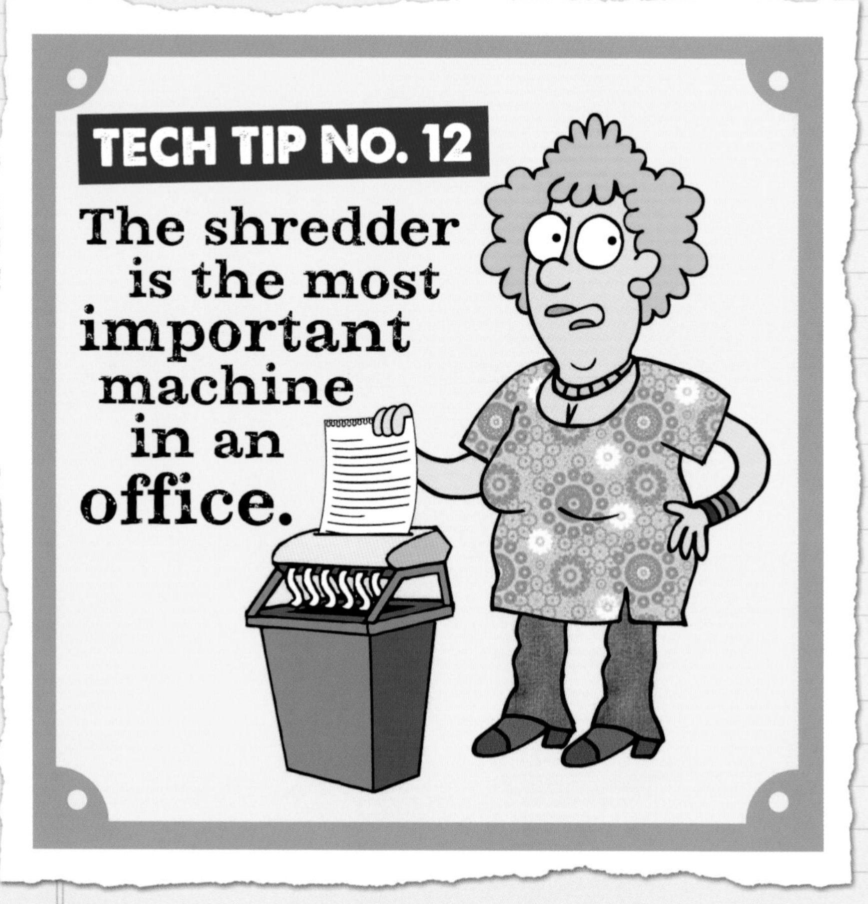
TECH TIP NO. 12
The shredder is the most important machine in an office.

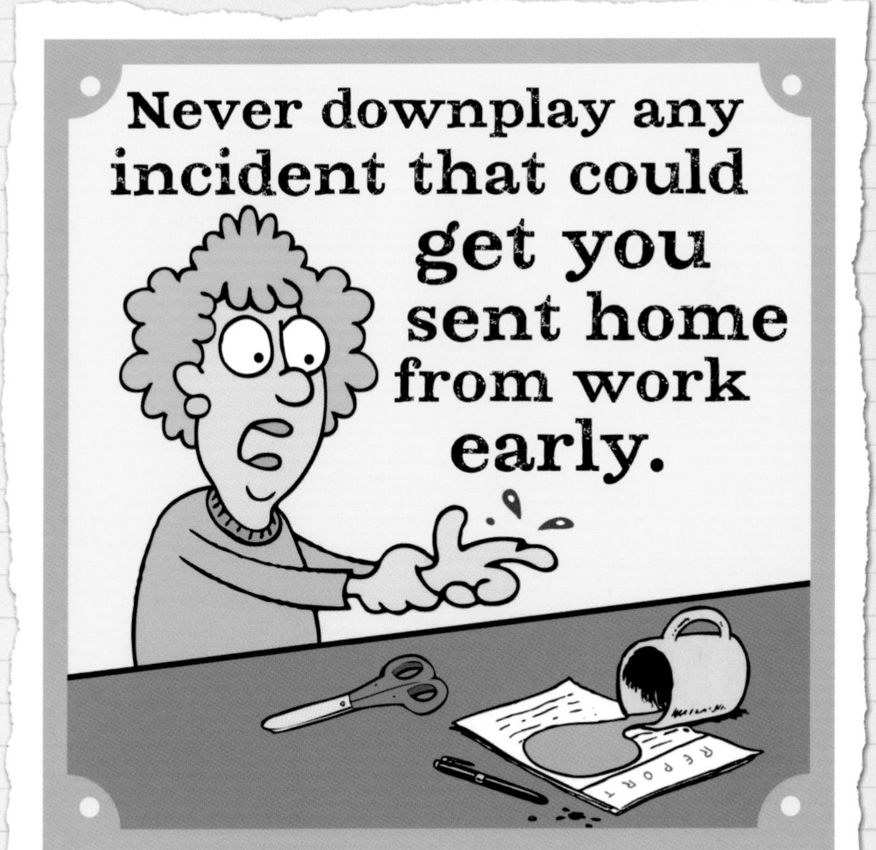
Never downplay any incident that could get you sent home from work early.
REPORT

When starting a **new job,** establish your **dominance** by putting the first person you see into a headlock.

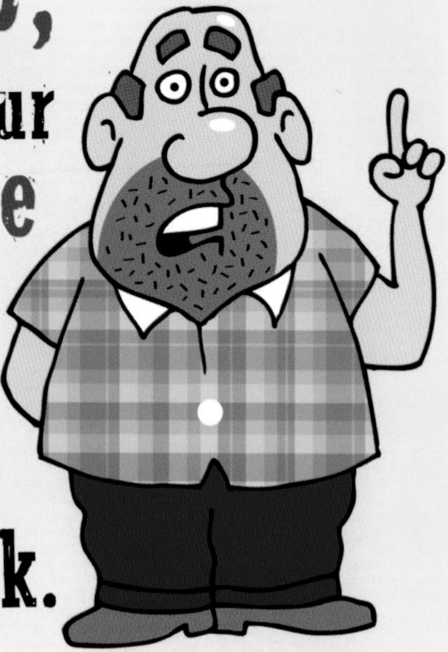

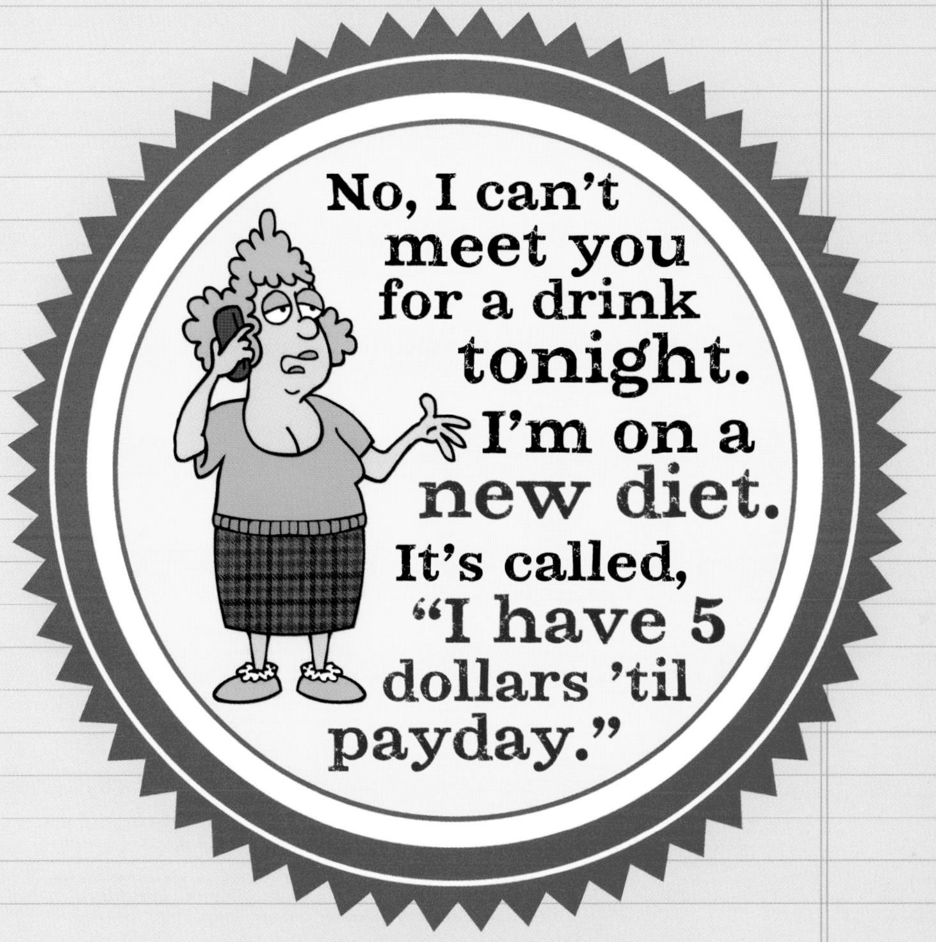
No, I can't meet you for a drink tonight.
I'm on a new diet.
It's called, "I have 5 dollars 'til payday."

Show me
a good
loser...

...and I'll show you a man playing golf with his boss.

We all have that one colleague who needs to learn how to whisper.

If you ever get caught sleeping at work, just lift your head and say, "And the Holy Spirit, Amen."

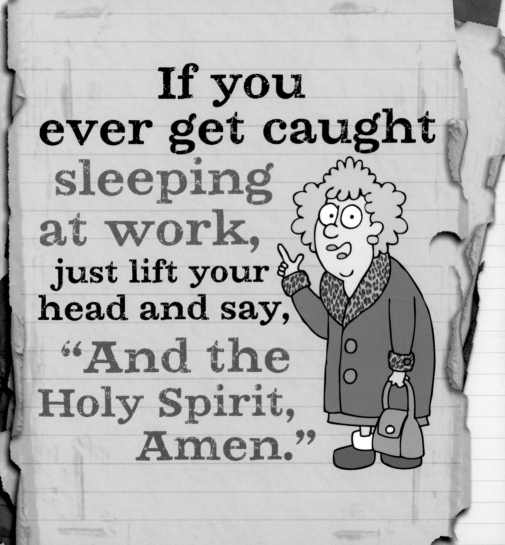

Remember when we were young and couldn't wait to grow up so we could do whatever we wanted, whenever we wanted?

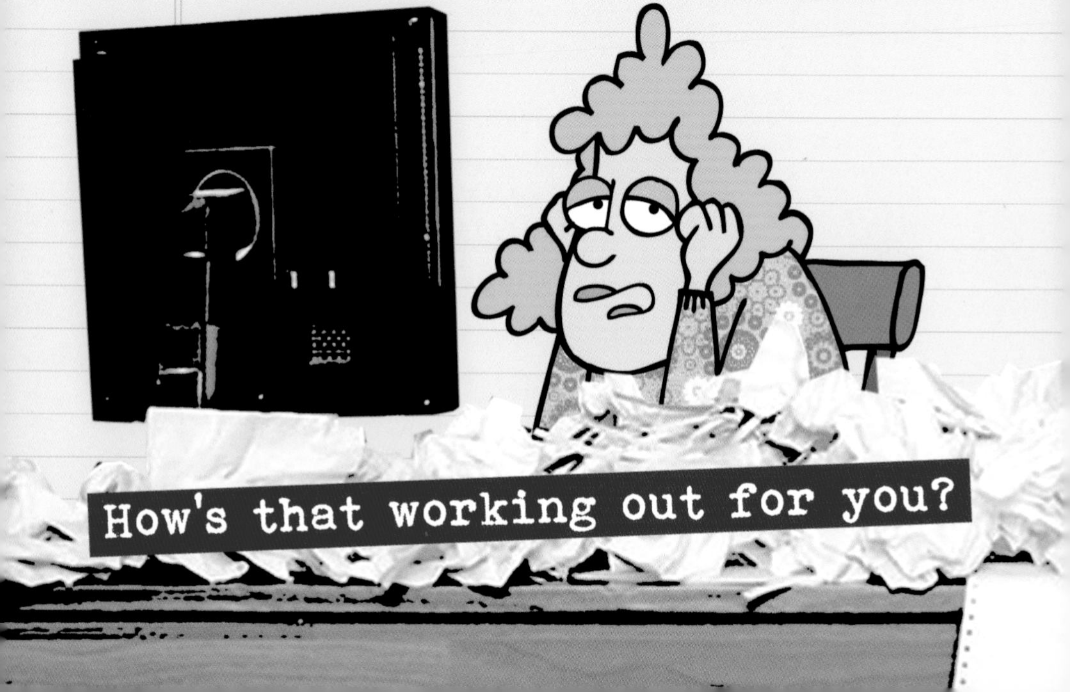
How's that working out for you?

You know
how you can hit
certain things a
few times to make
them work again?

I wish I could do
that with certain
colleagues!

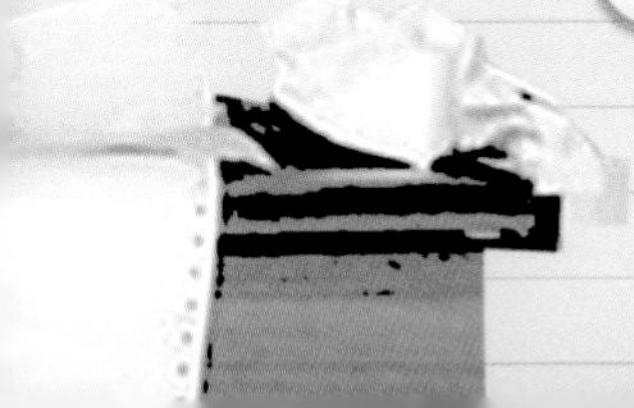

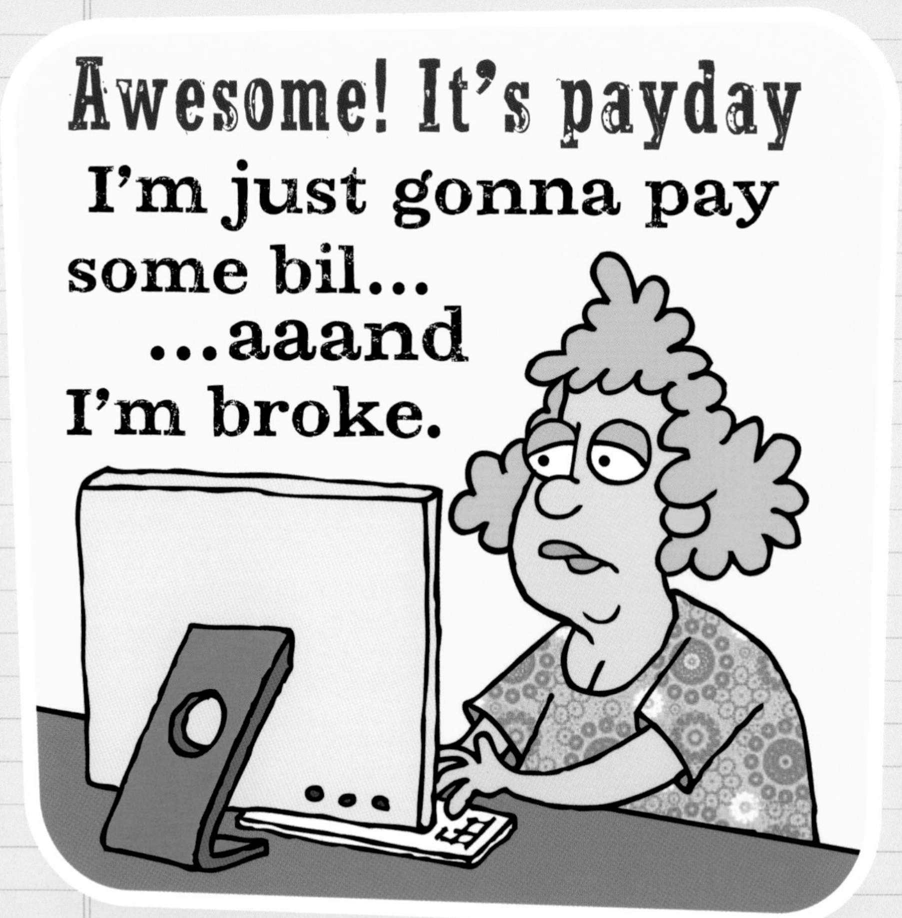
Awesome! It's payday
I'm just gonna pay
some bil...
...aaand
I'm broke.

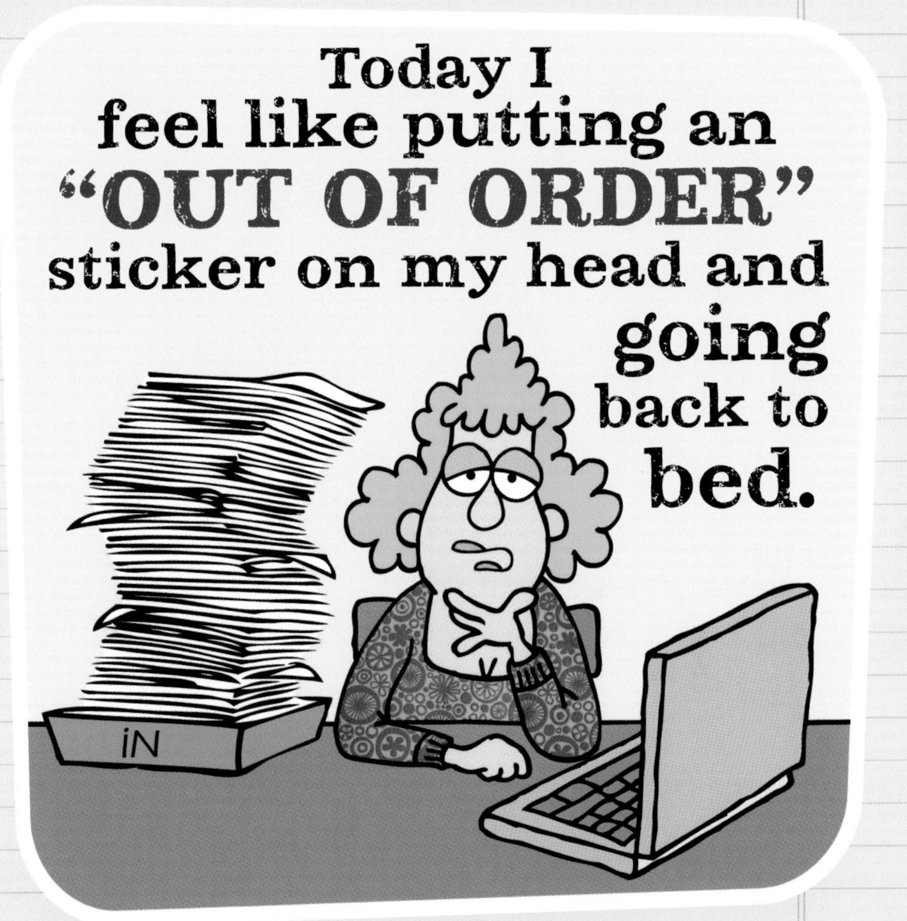
Today I feel like putting an "OUT OF ORDER" sticker on my head and going back to bed.
iN

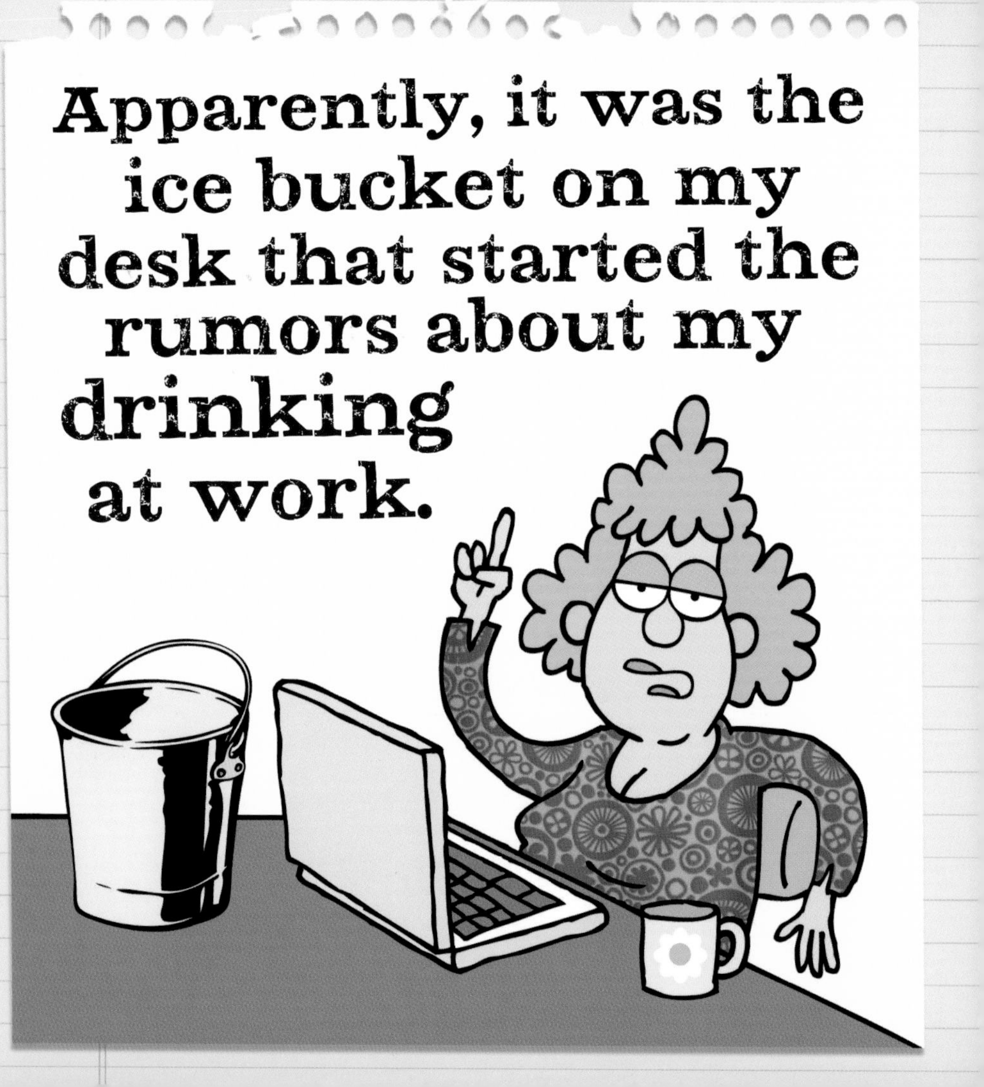
Apparently, it was the ice bucket on my desk that started the rumors about my drinking at work.

AUNTY ACID OFFICE TIP

NO. 23

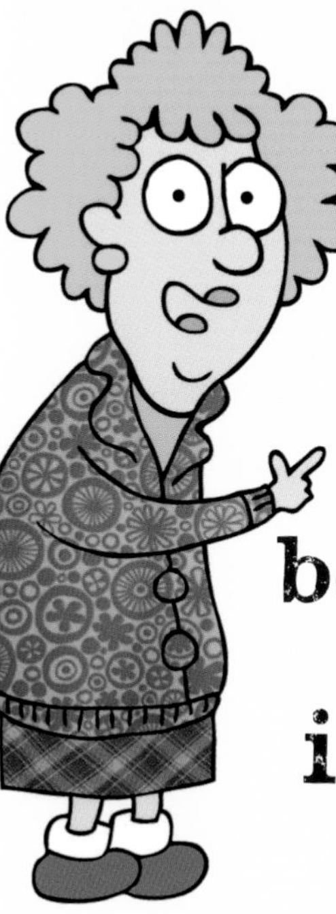

If you put a blob of **BLU-TACK** on your booze bottle, it doesn't roll around in your desk drawer.

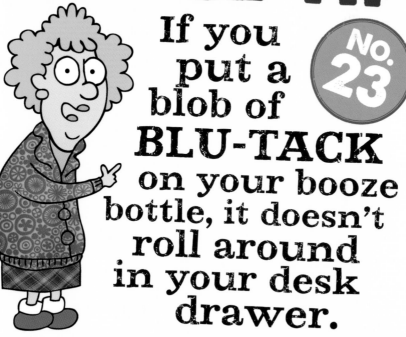

I hit my target at work and got fired.

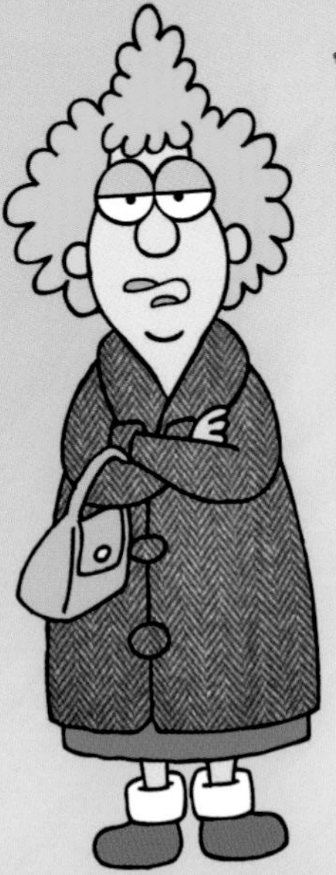

I'm not too bothered though…

she had it coming.

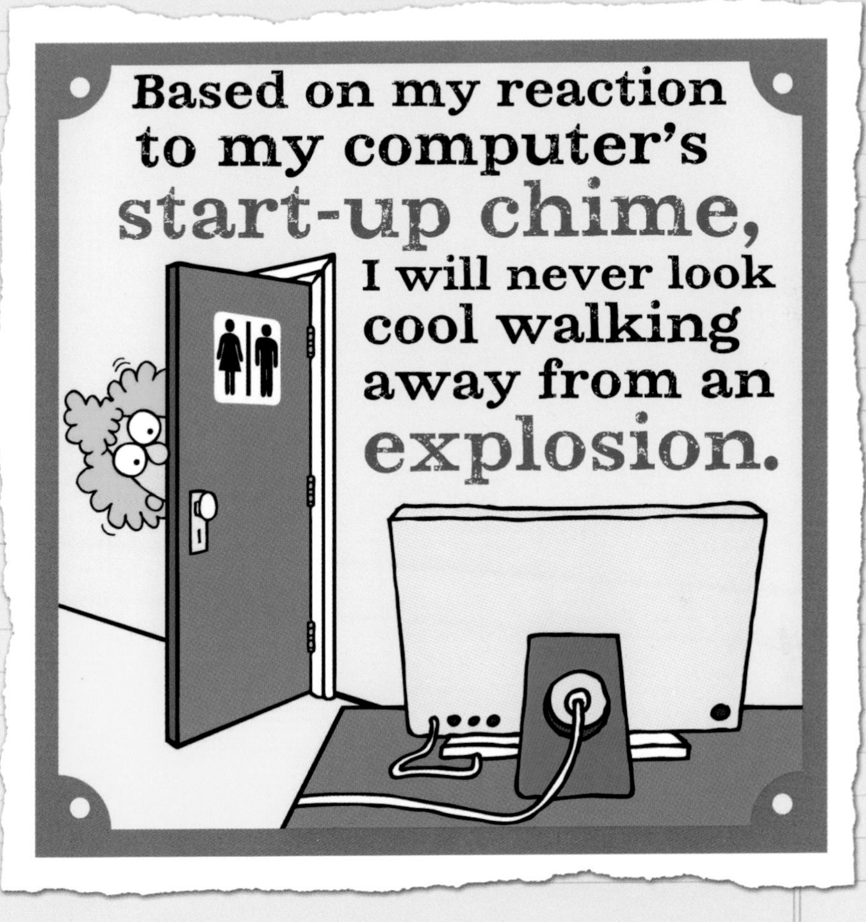
Based on my reaction
to my computer's
start-up chime,
I will never look
cool walking
away from an
explosion.

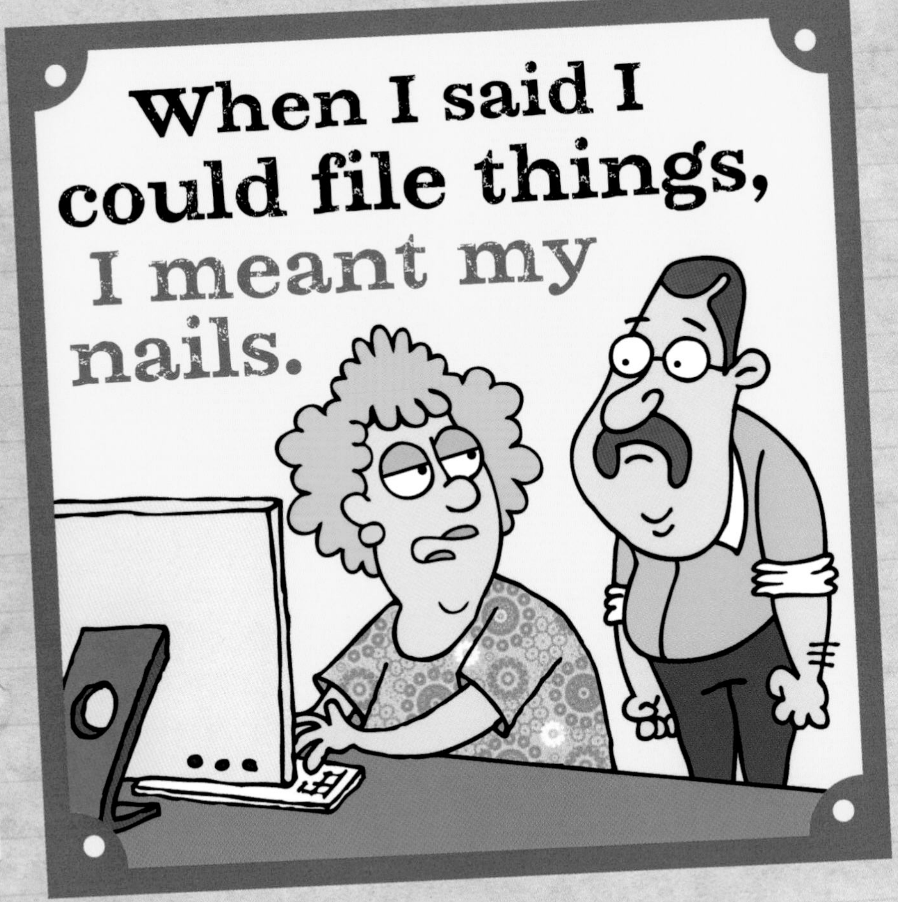
When I said I
could file things,
I meant my
nails.

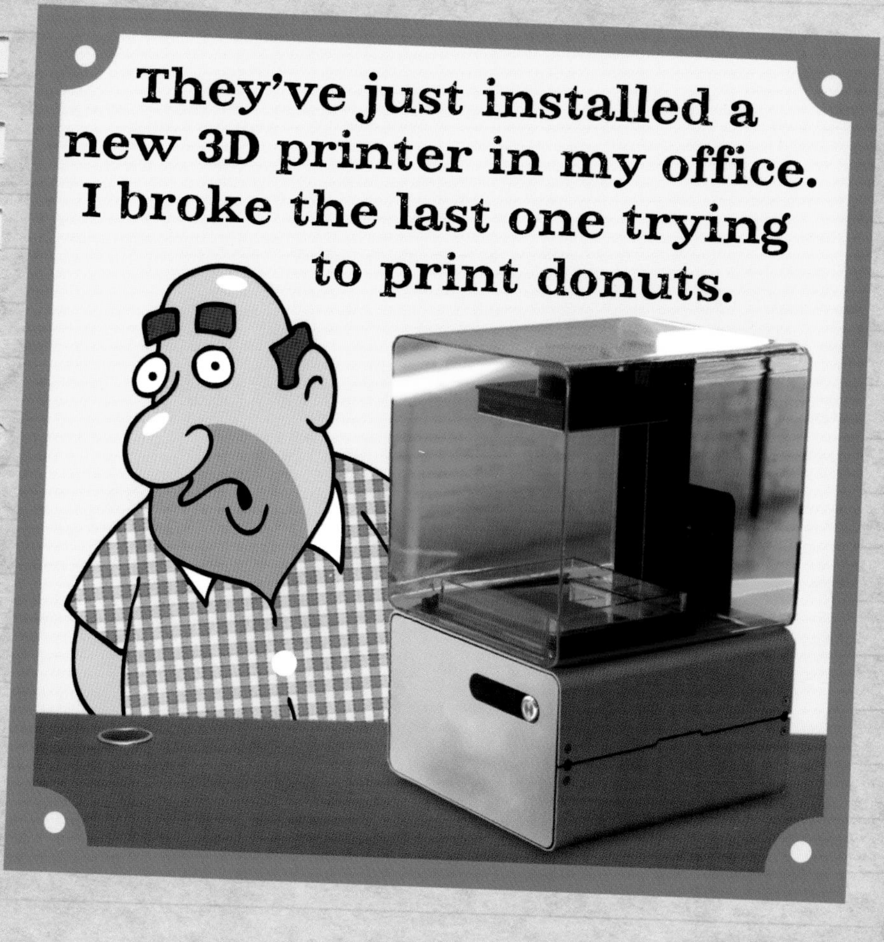
They've just installed a new 3D printer in my office. I broke the last one trying to print donuts.

Apparently, HR wants a word with me about my attendance.

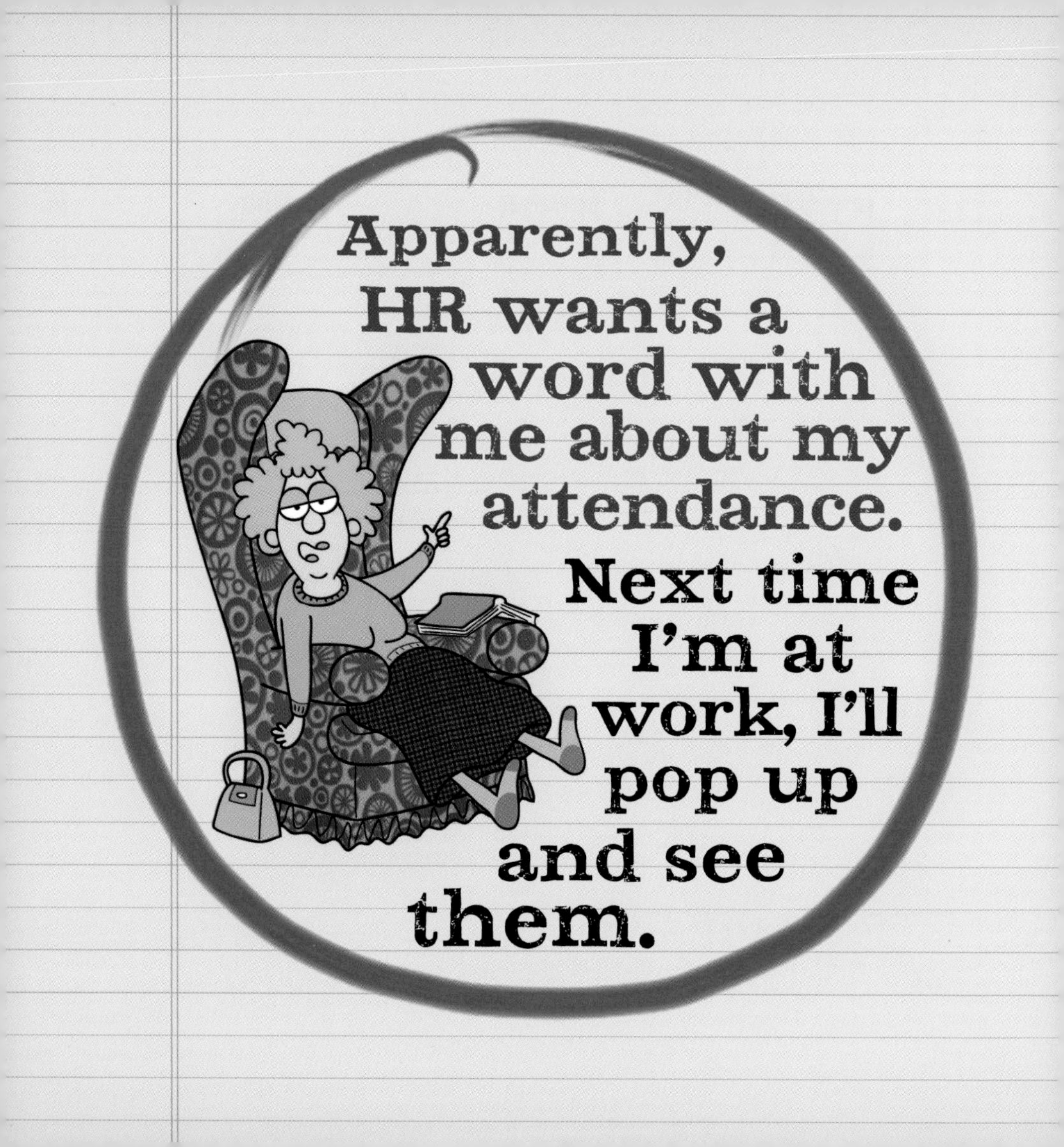

Next time I'm at work, I'll pop up and see them.

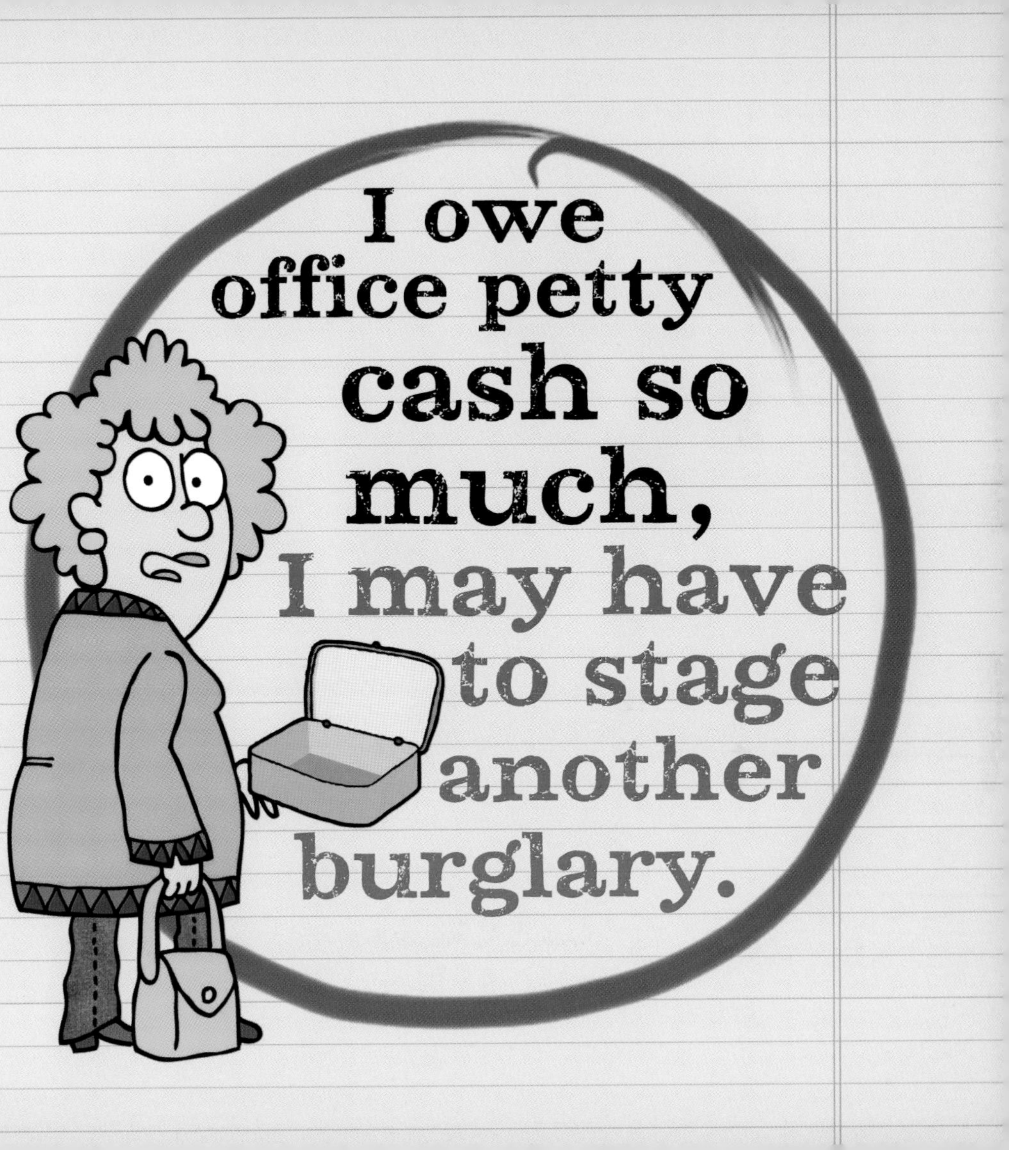

I owe office petty cash so much, I may have to stage another burglary.

If cleanliness is next to Godliness, then my office must be a portal to Hell.

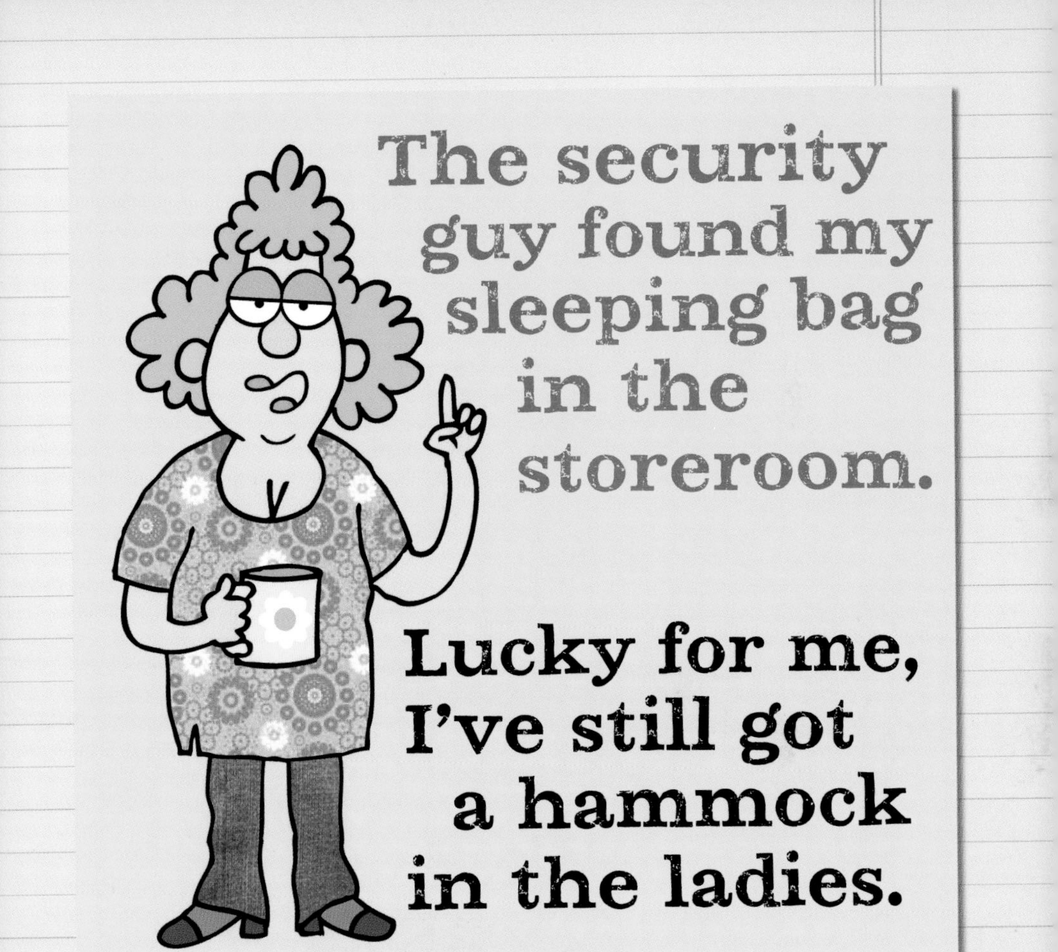

The security guy found my sleeping bag in the storeroom.

Lucky for me, I've still got a hammock in the ladies.

If you think **you're** bad at your job, spare a thought for this guy.

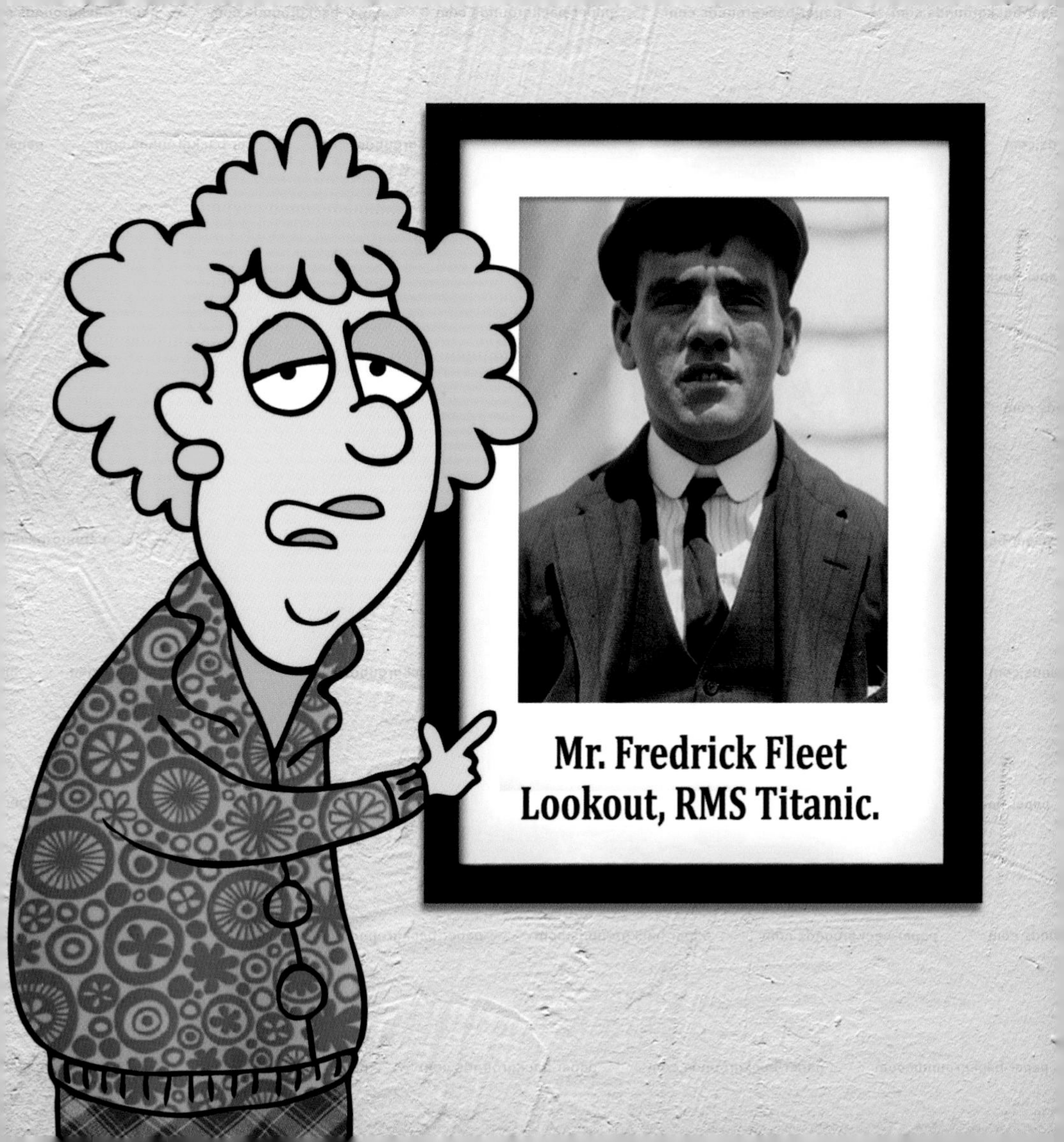
Mr. Fredrick Fleet
Lookout, RMS Titanic.

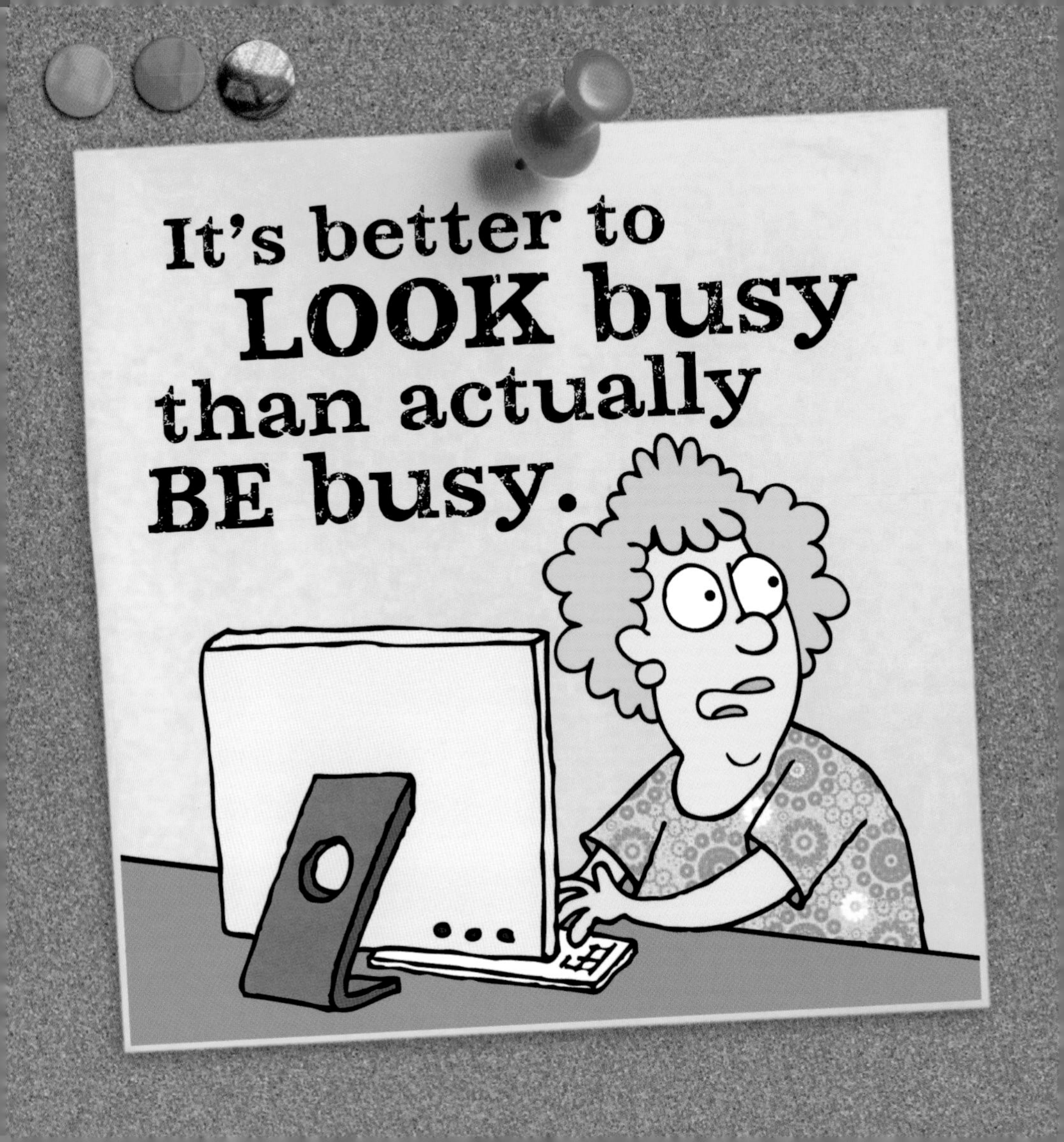
It's better to
LOOK busy
than actually
BE busy.

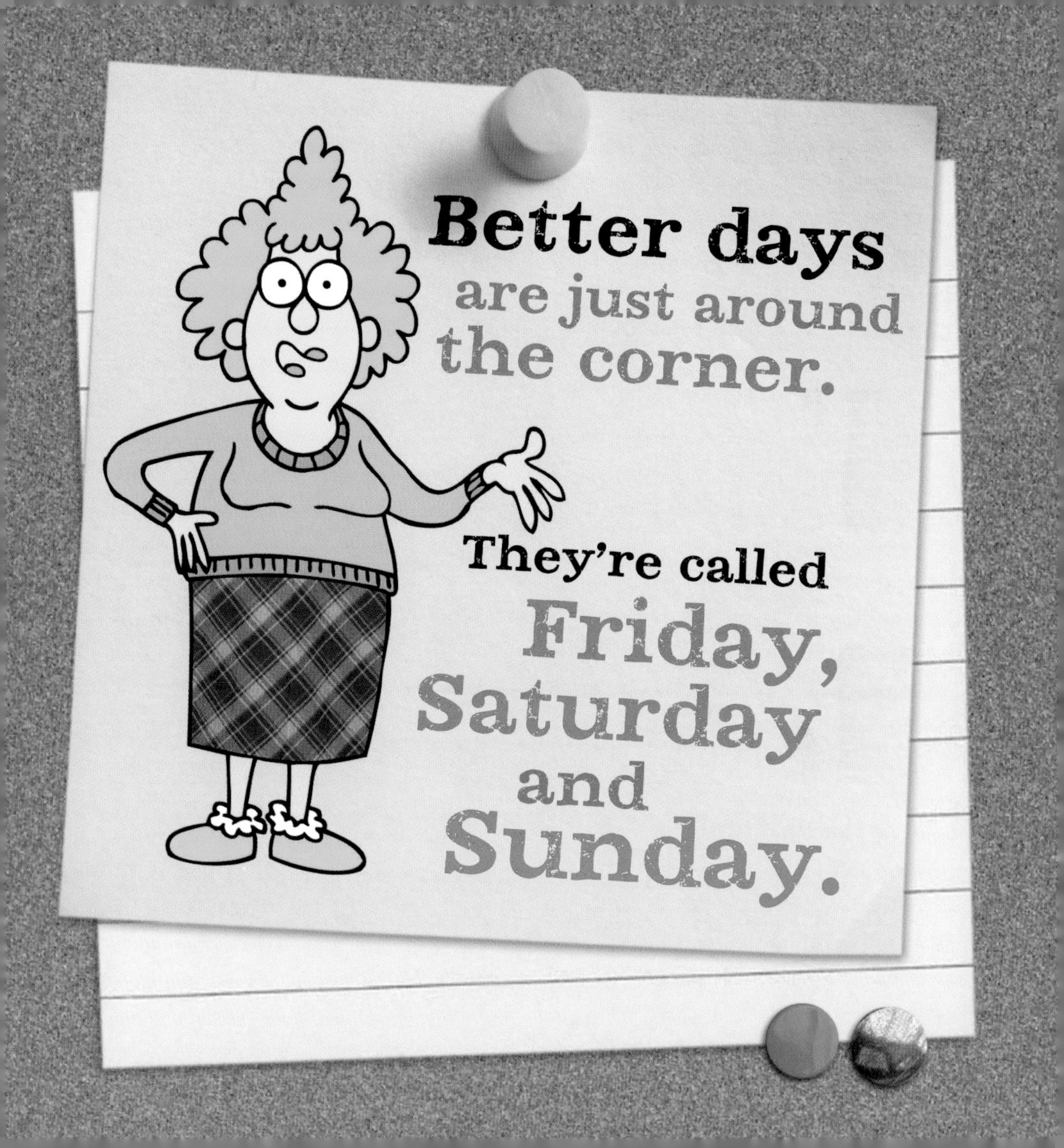

Better days
are just around
the corner.

They're called
Friday,
Saturday
and
Sunday.

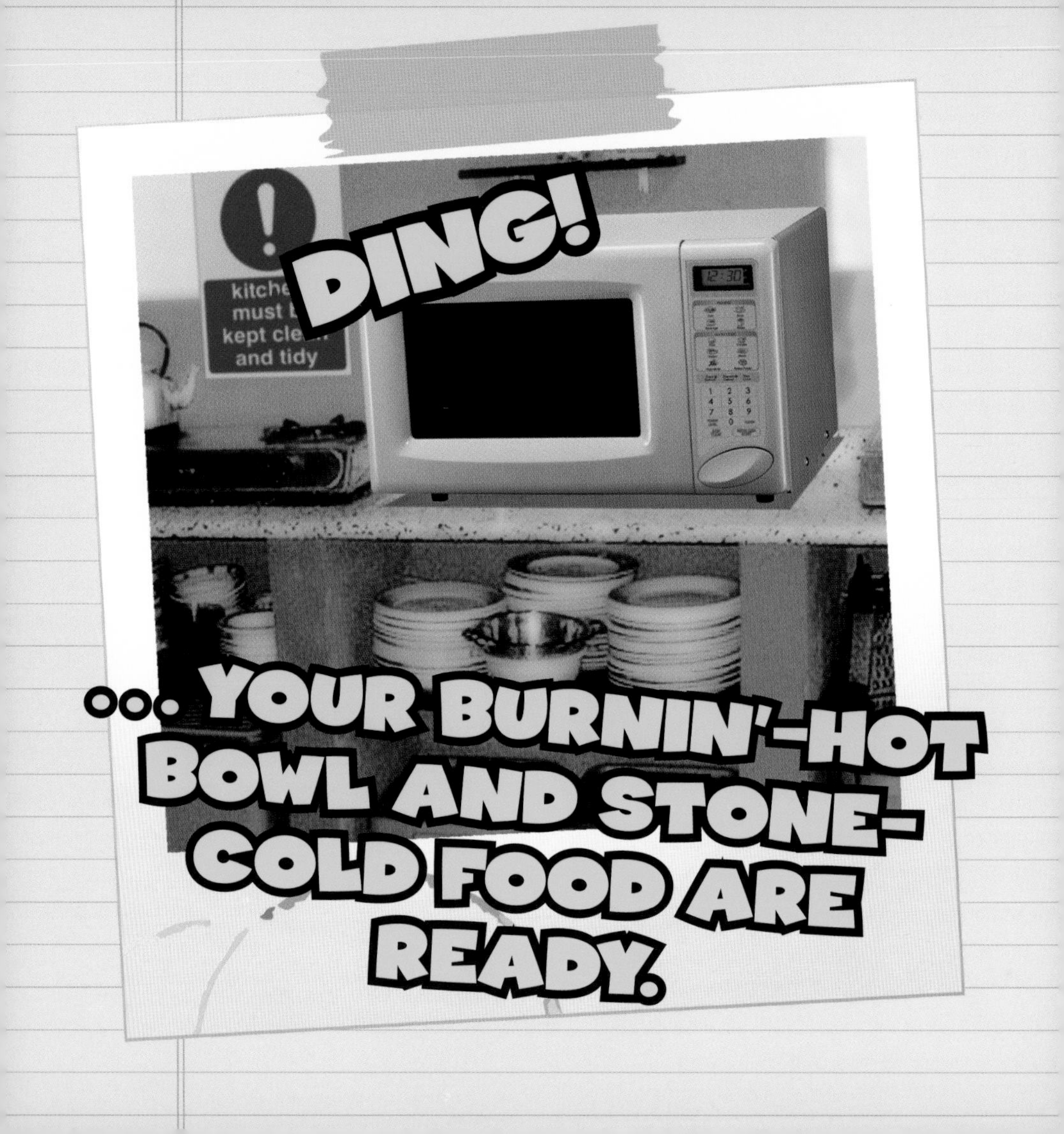
and tidy

DING!

... YOUR BURNIN'-HOT BOWL AND STONE-COLD FOOD ARE READY.

By my reckoning, it's "Don't-give-a-crap" o'clock.

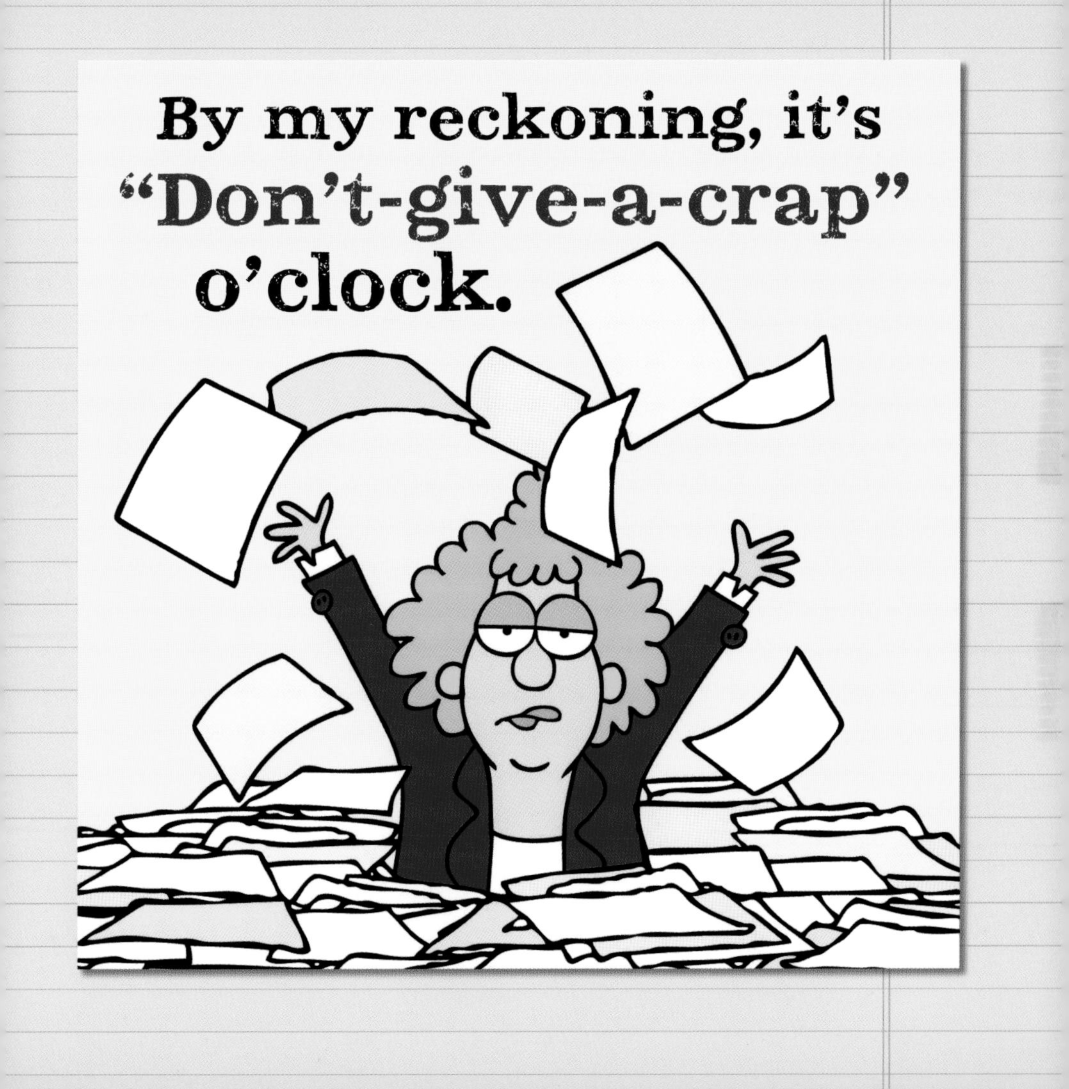

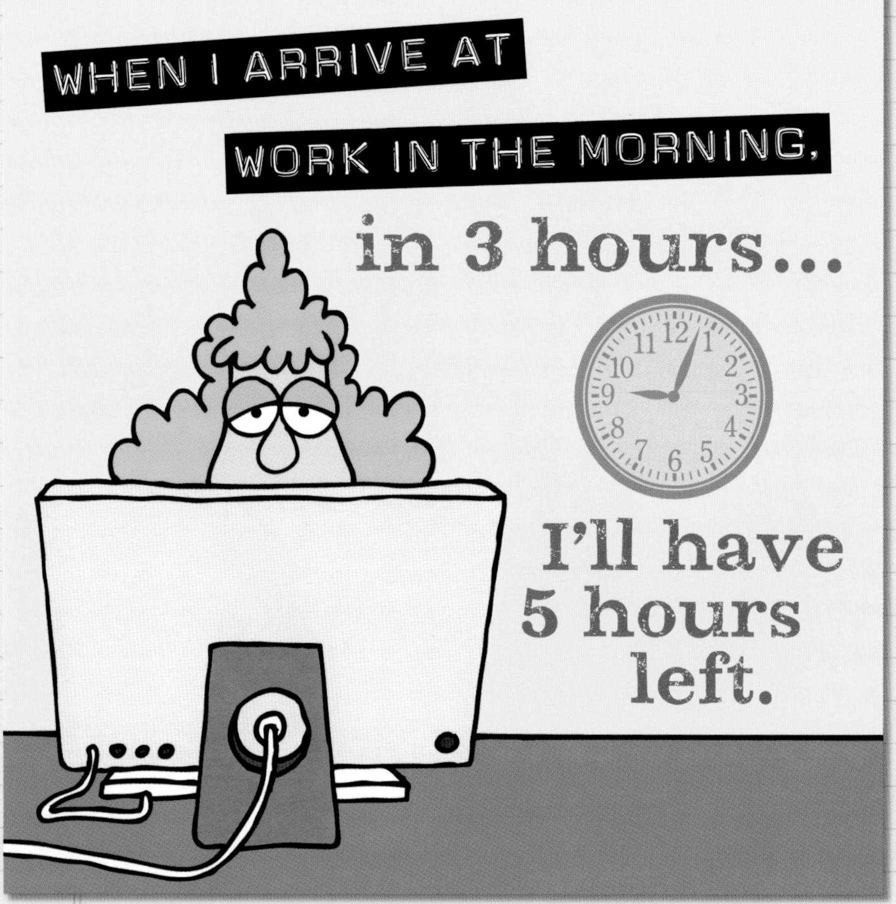

WHEN I ARRIVE AT
WORK IN THE MORNING,
in 3 hours...
I'll have
5 hours
left.

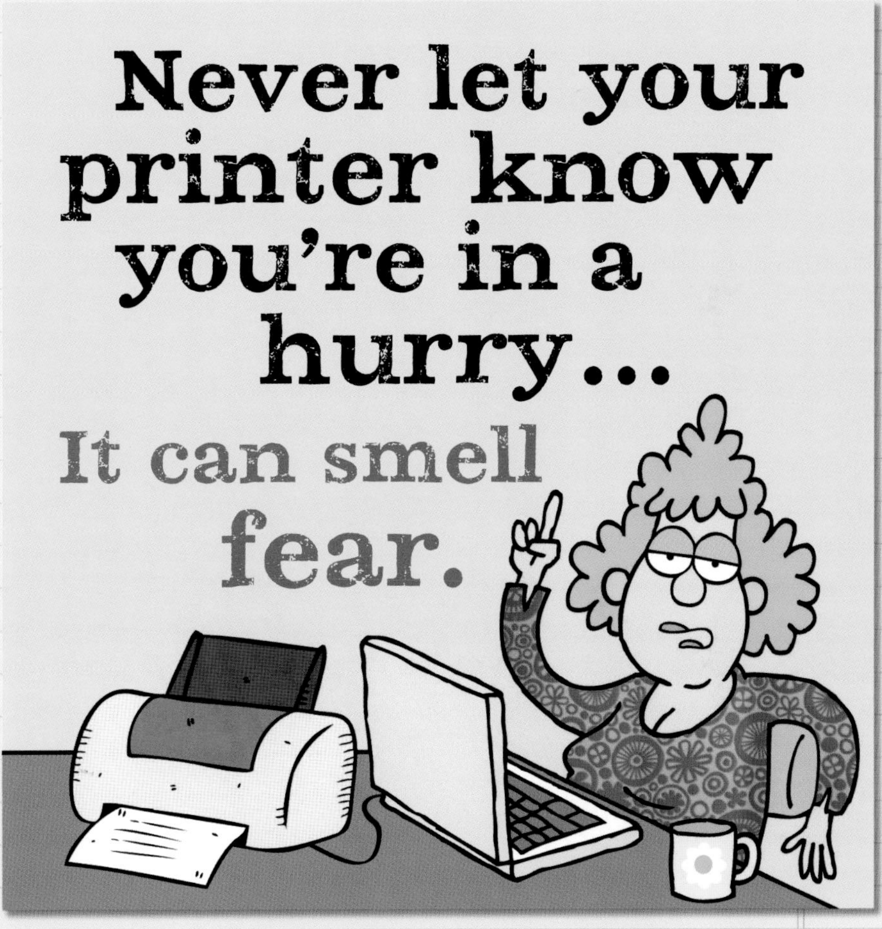
Never let your printer know you're in a hurry...
It can smell fear.

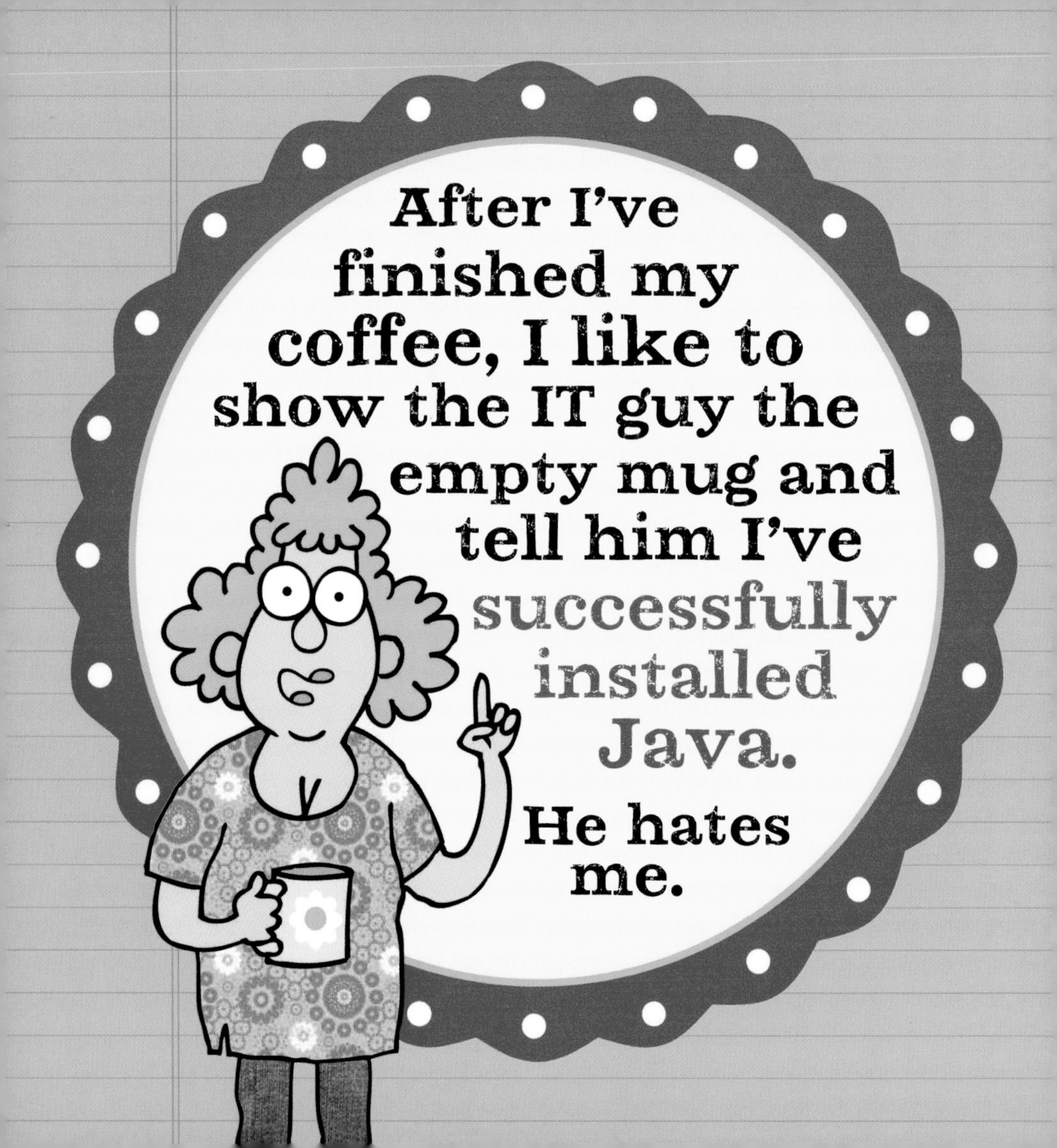
After I've finished my coffee, I like to show the IT guy the empty mug and tell him I've successfully installed Java.
He hates me.

There's a moron in every office... and they generally get paid a lot more than you.

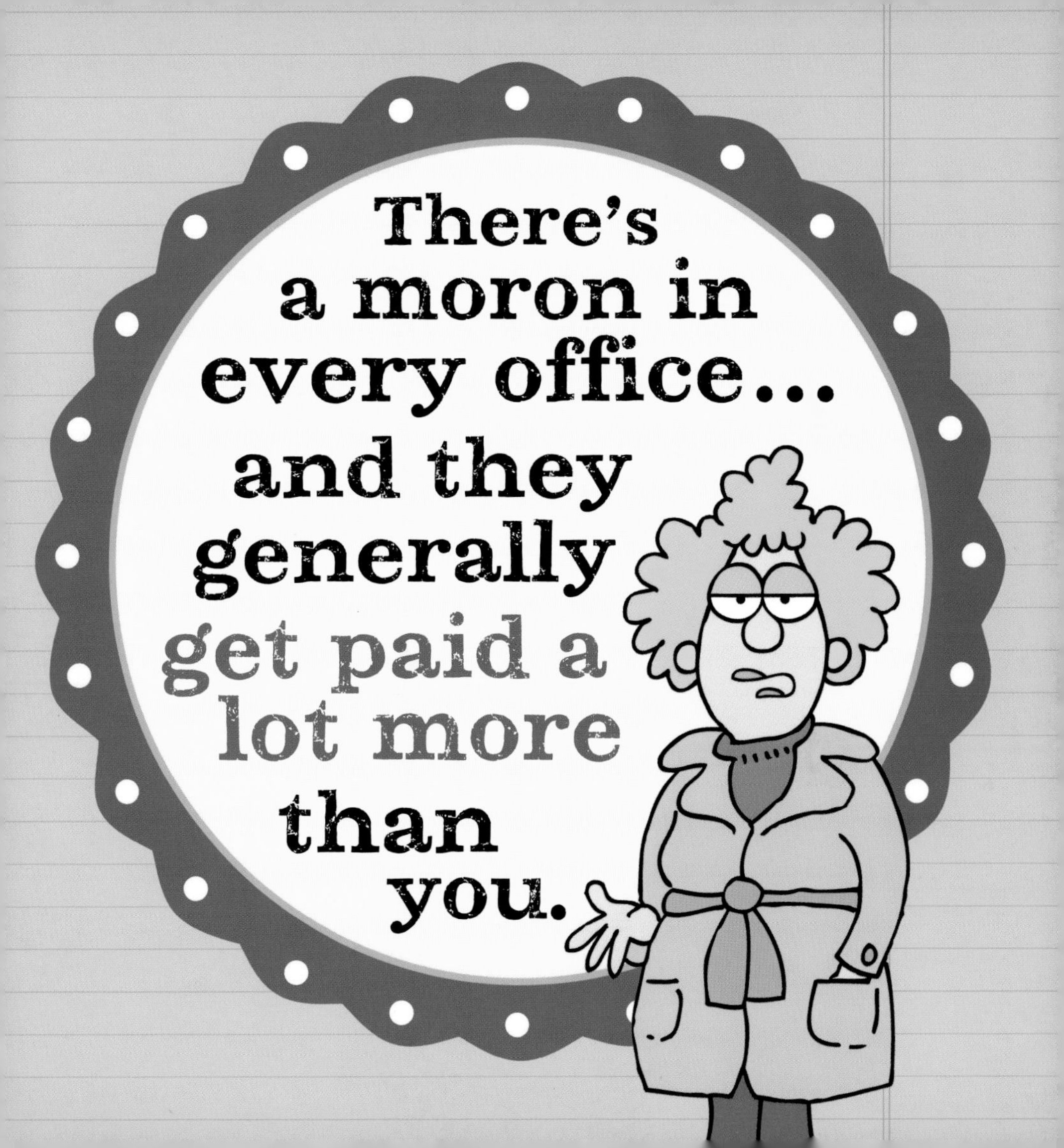

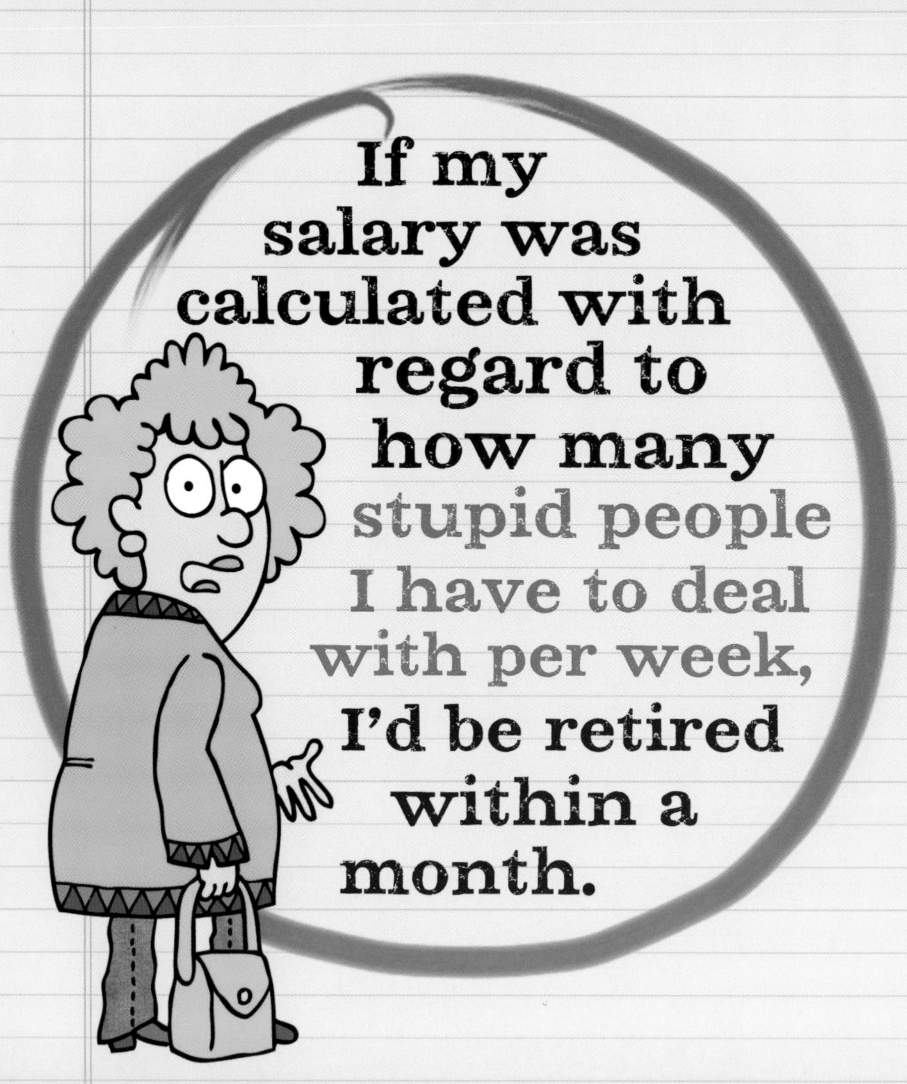

If my salary was calculated with regard to how many stupid people I have to deal with per week, I'd be retired within a month.

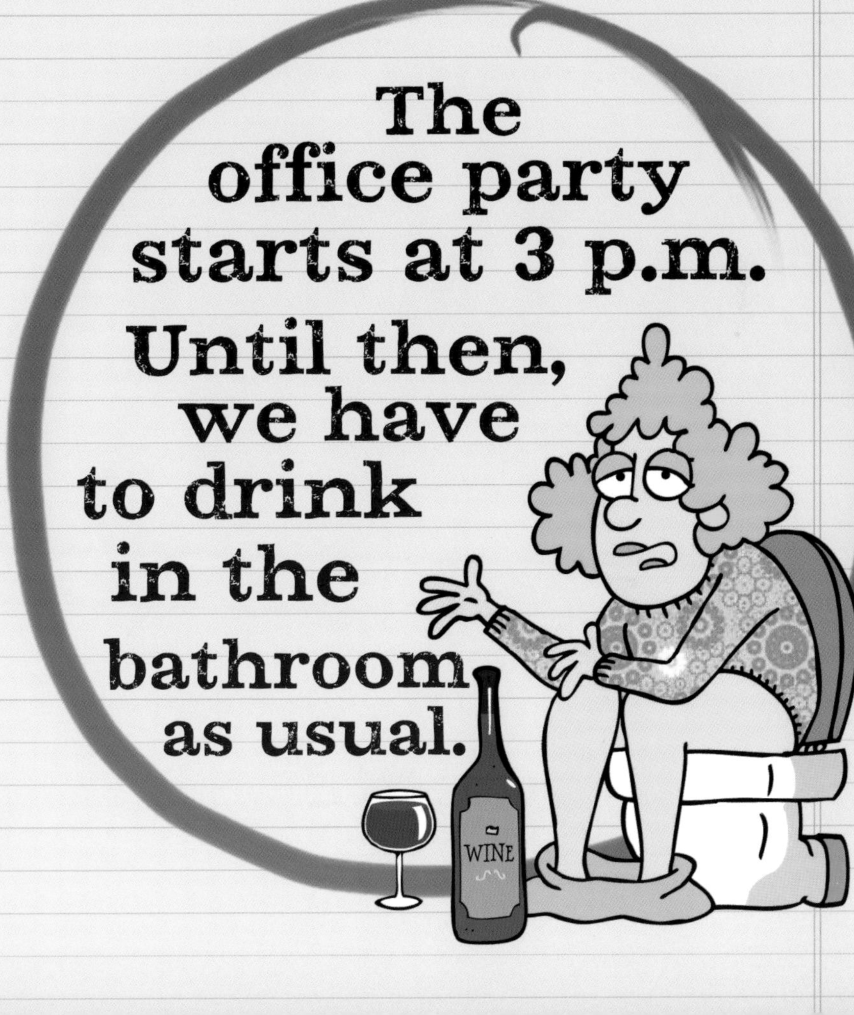
The office party starts at 3 p.m.
Until then, we have to drink in the bathroom as usual.
WINE

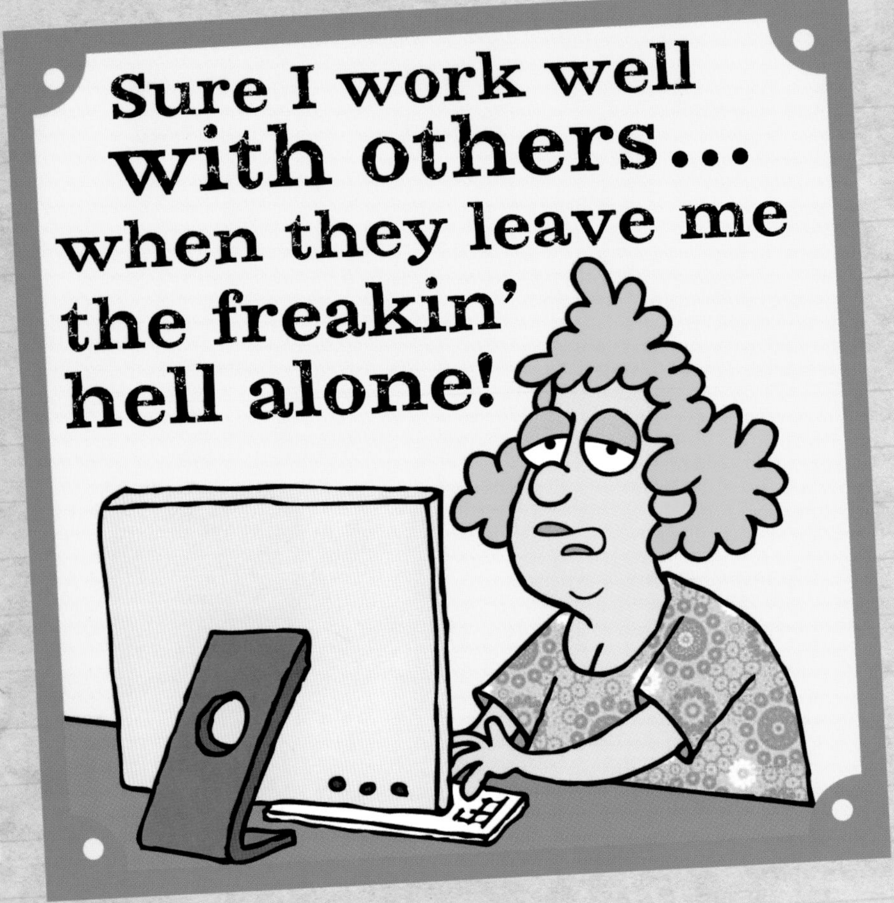
Sure I work well
with others...
when they leave me
the freakin'
hell alone!

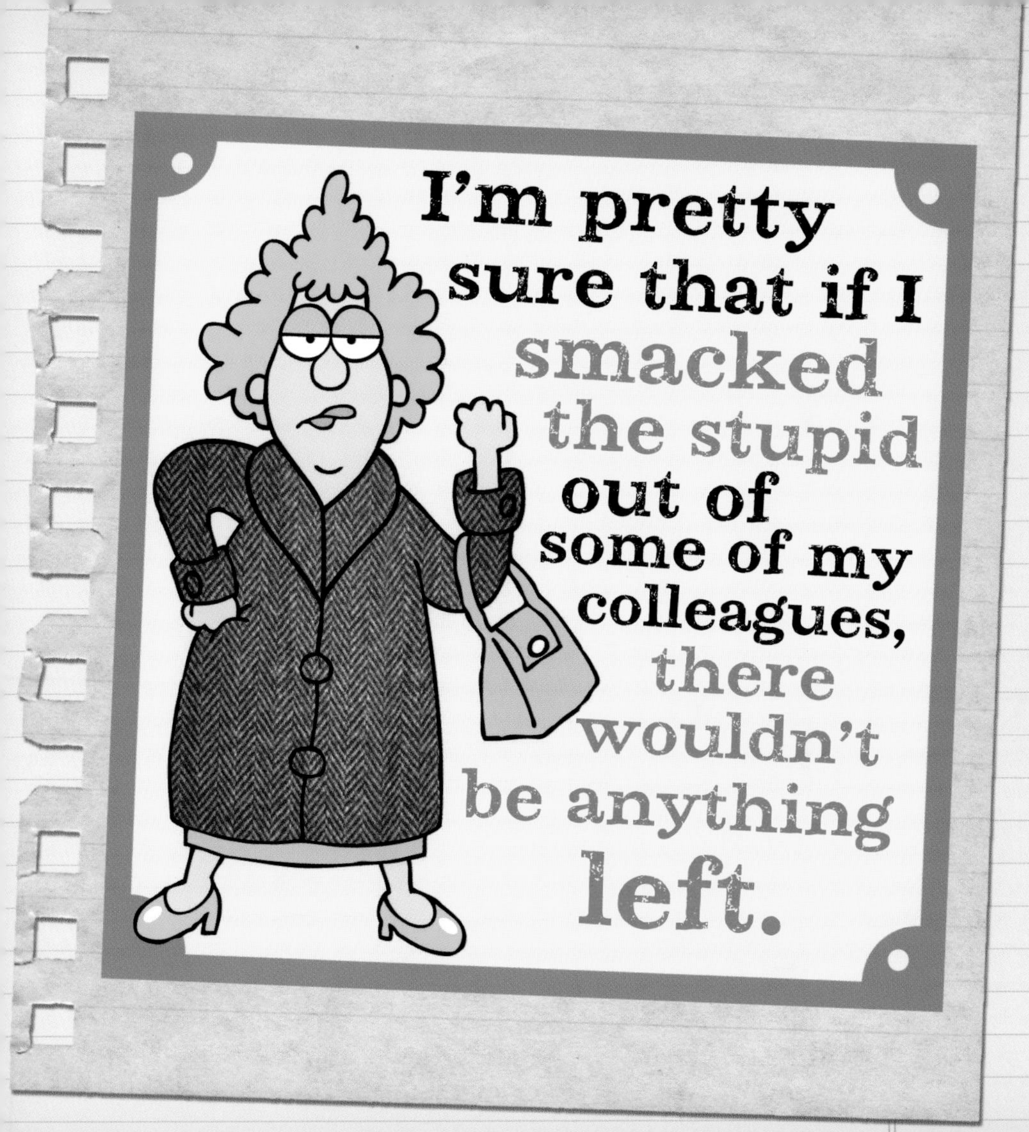

I'm pretty sure that if I smacked the stupid out of some of my colleagues, there wouldn't be anything left.

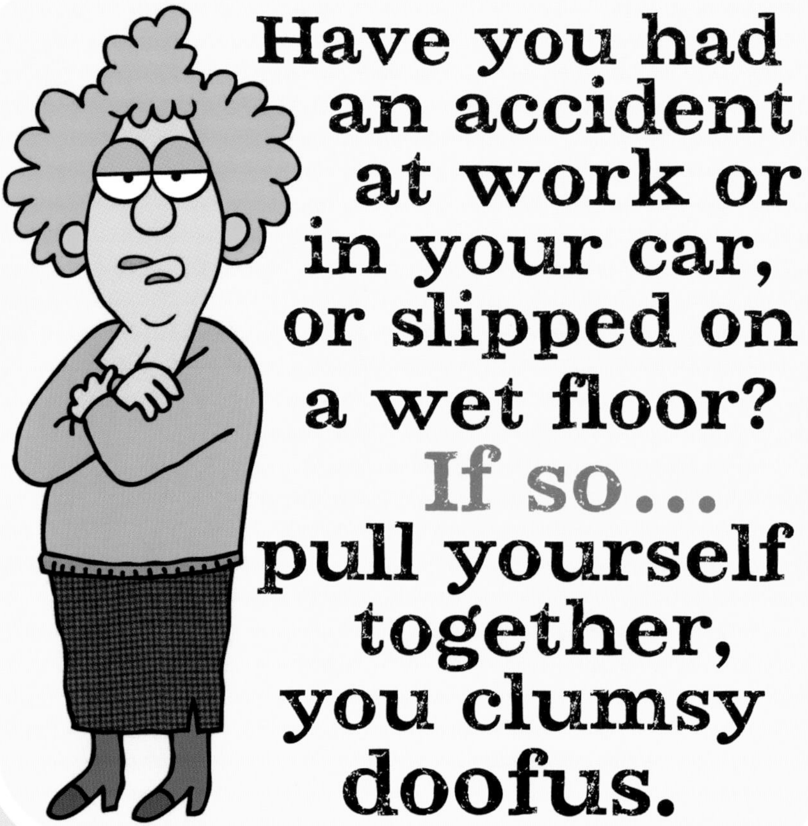

Have you had an accident at work or in your car, or slipped on a wet floor?

If so...

pull yourself together, you clumsy doofus.

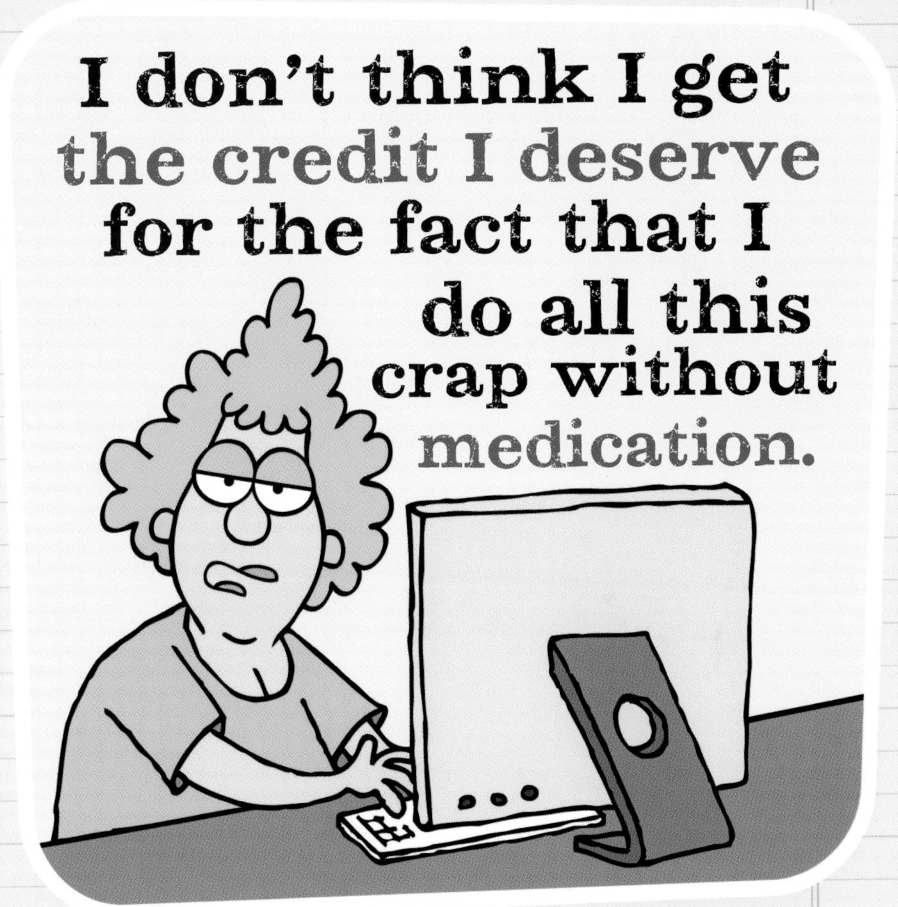
I don't think I get
the credit I deserve
for the fact that I
do all this
crap without
medication.

Every time I think I've got all my ducks in a row,

the darn things start waddling off in different directions!

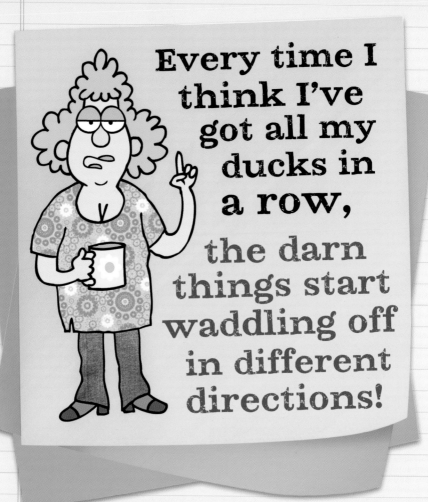

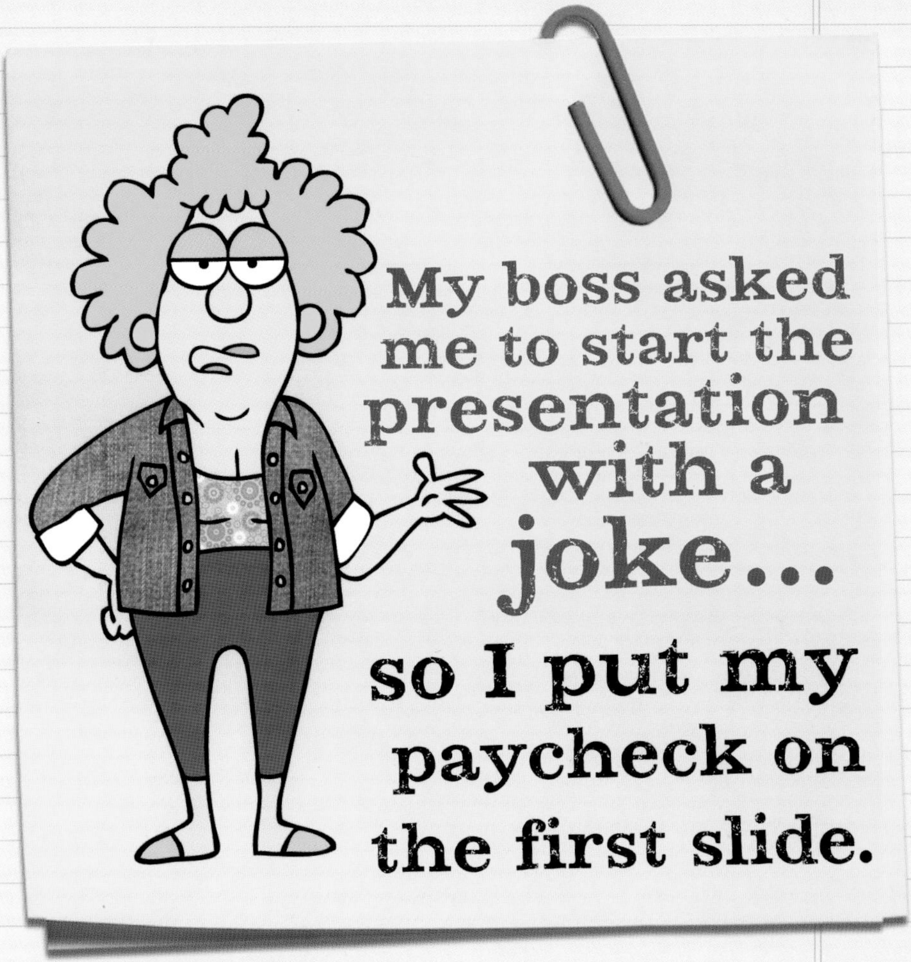
My boss asked me to start the presentation with a joke...
so I put my paycheck on the first slide.

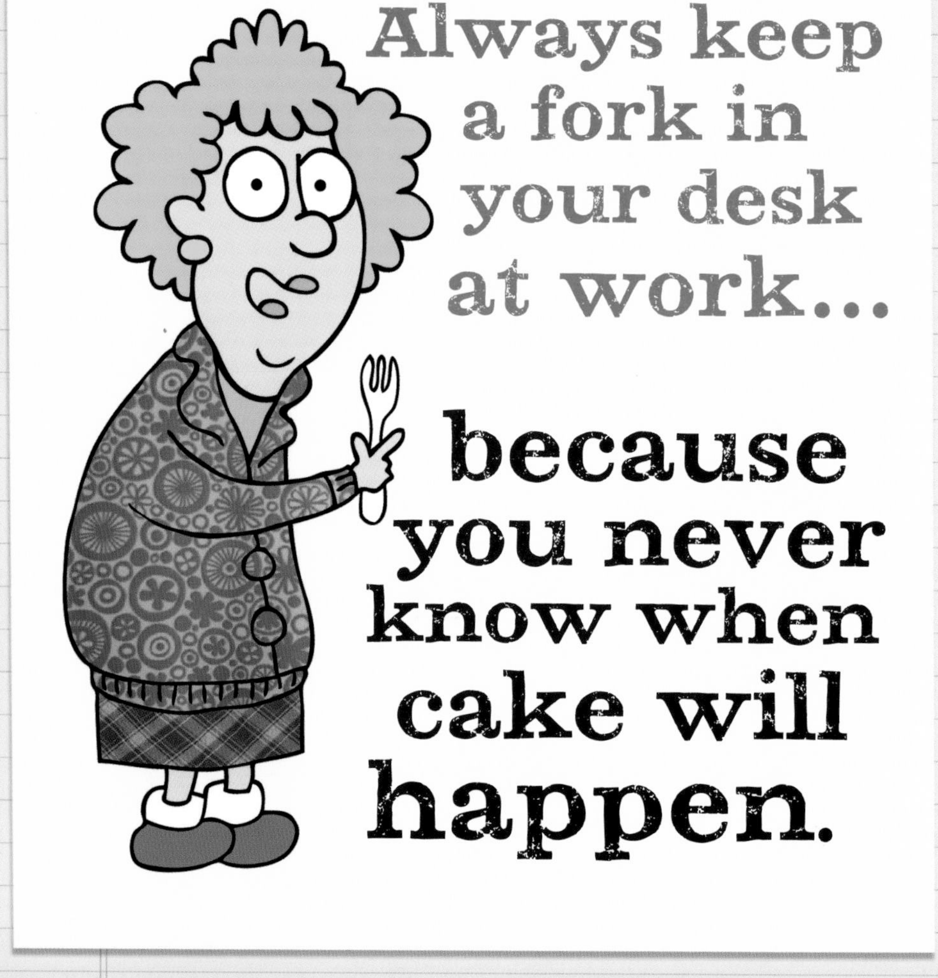

Always keep a fork in your desk at work...

because you never know when cake will happen.

I took a cab to work the other day and the driver said to me, "I love my job. I own this car, I've got my own business, I'm my own boss and no one tells me what to do."

I said, "Turn left, here."

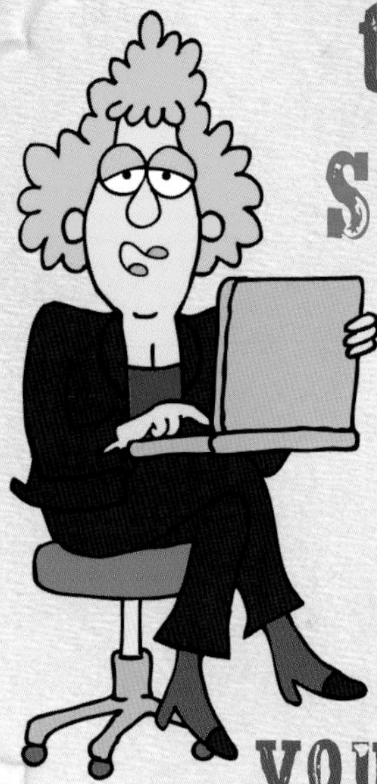

Be nice to your secretary. They know ALL your secrets.

I've heard about history repeating itself... but this "Monday" thing has to stop.

Of course **women** don't work as hard **as men.**

They get it right the first time.

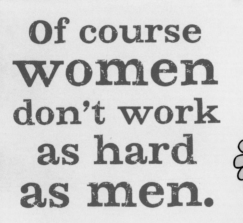

A dangerous virus called "Weekly Overload Recreational Killer" (WORK) is currently infecting lots of people.

If you become exposed to the virus, go quickly to the nearest "Biological Anxiety Relief" (BAR) establishment and ask the staff for the following antidotes: "Work Isolating Neutralizer Extract" (WINE) and "Bothersome Employer Elimination Remedy" (BEER).

MY TOP OFFICE POST-IT NOTES

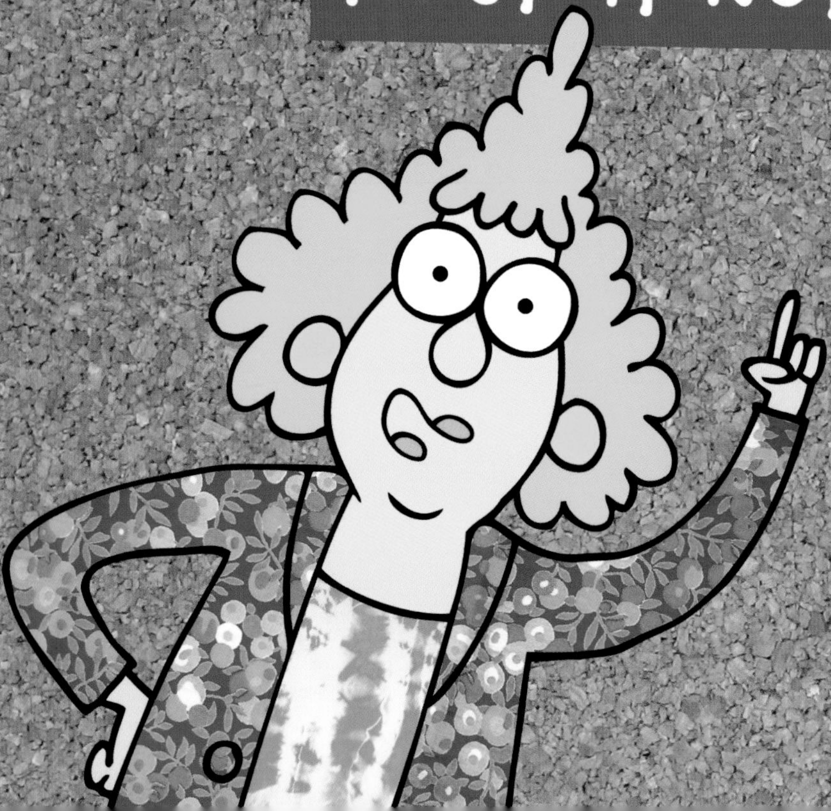

I've popped out to get ammo xxxx
Stop washing your feet in the toilet!
If the cops do come don't let them look in my desk drawers
It was raining, so I stole your coat

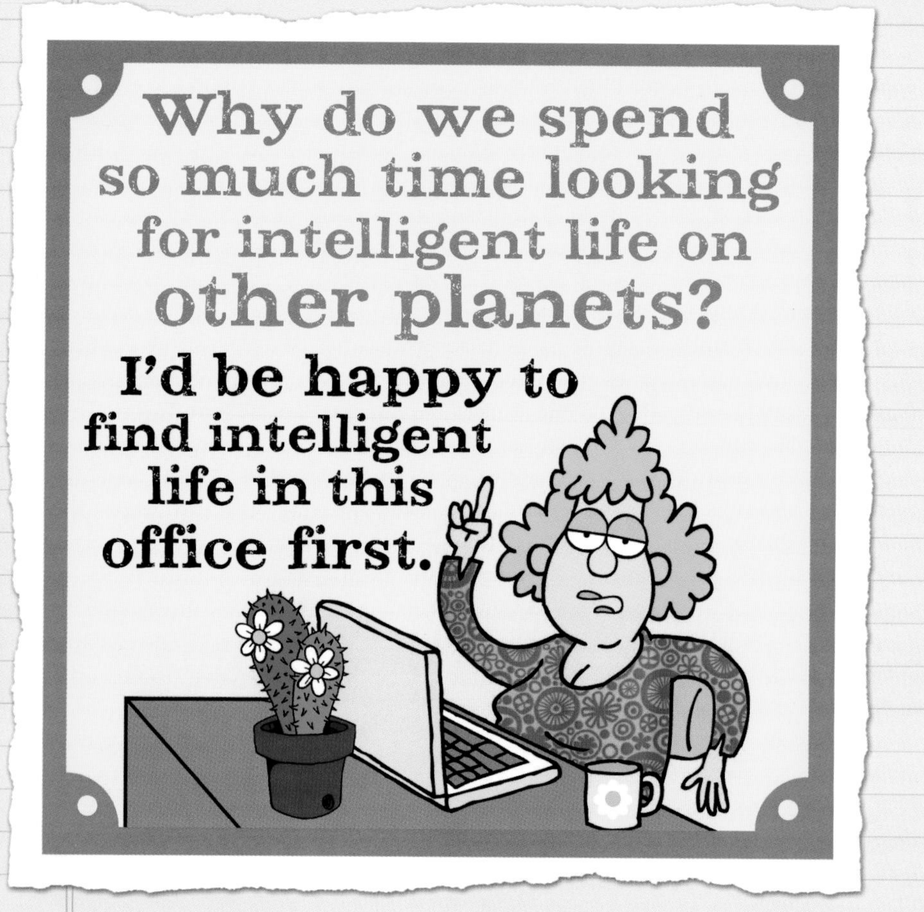
Why do we spend so much time looking for intelligent life on other planets?
I'd be happy to find intelligent life in this office first.

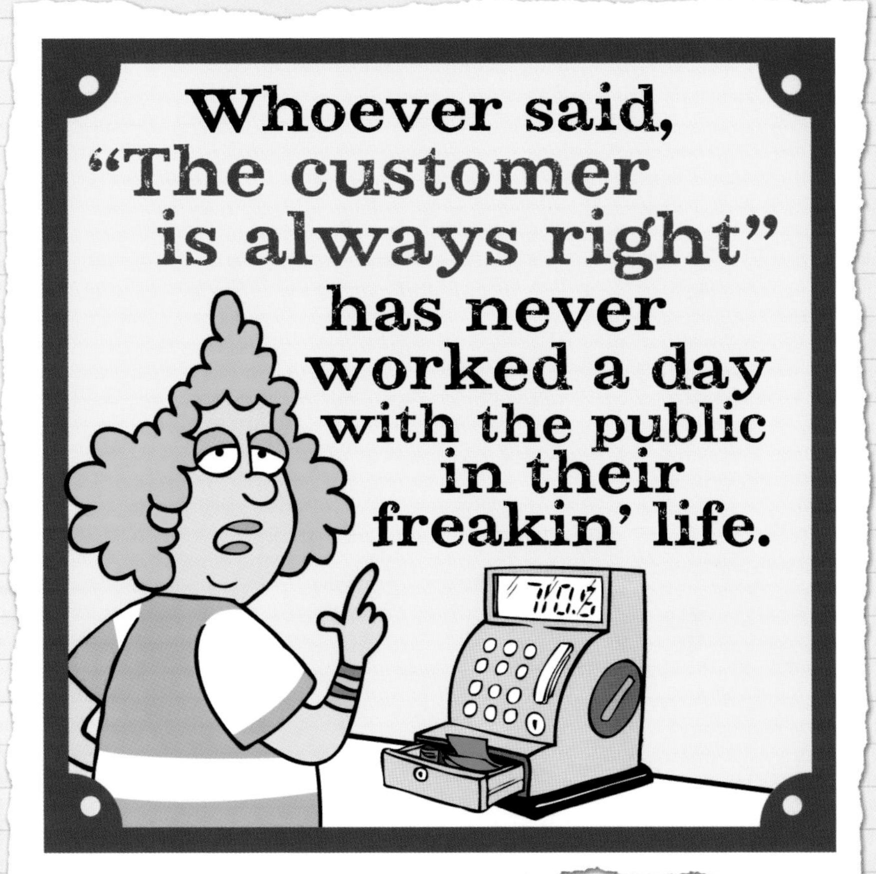
Whoever said,
"The customer
is always right"
has never
worked a day
with the public
in their
freakin' life.

They say that success is doing what you love and making it a career.

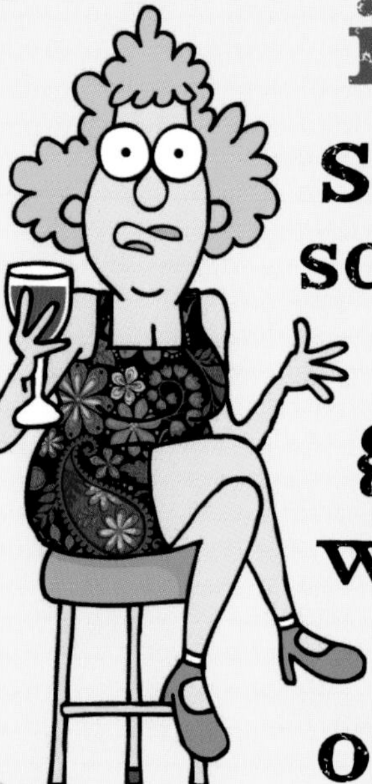

So I need to find someone who'll pay me to guzzle wine while looking at funny pictures of cats online.

I've just made it through a full day at work without beating someone with a chair.

I'd say my people skills are definitely improving.

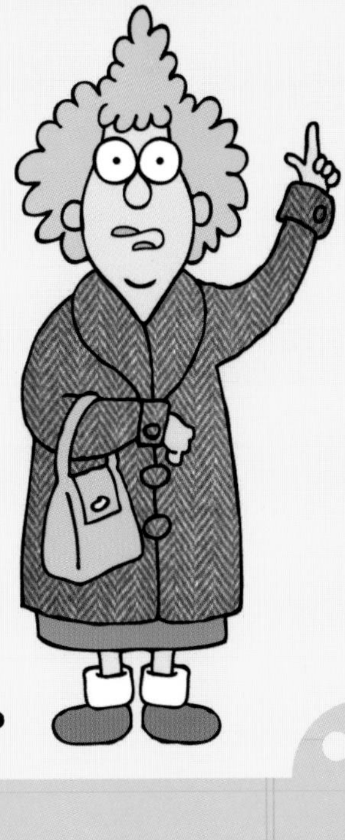

It’s been that kind of day...

just keep pouring.

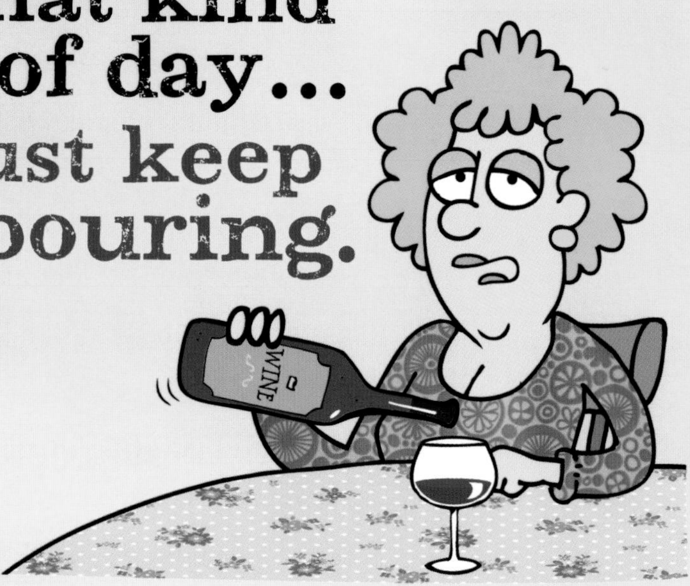
WINE

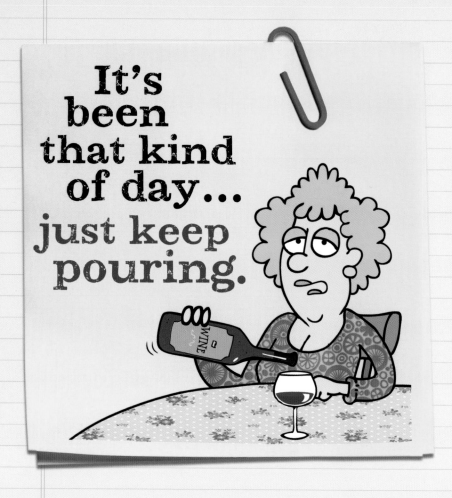

When they said they were getting a robot to cover my leave, I must admit I was expecting something a little more high-tech.

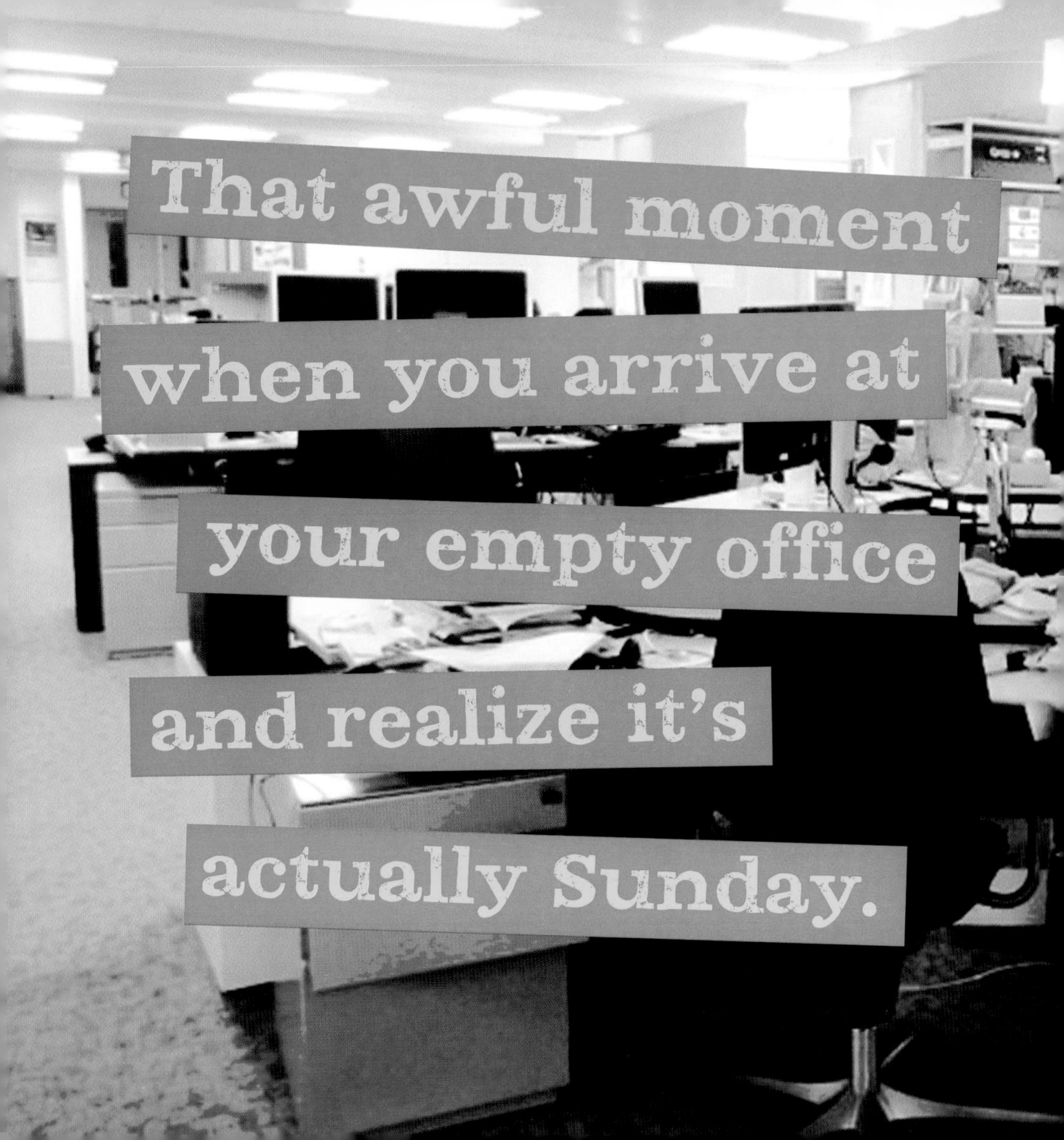
That awful moment
when you arrive at
your empty office
and realize it's
actually Sunday.

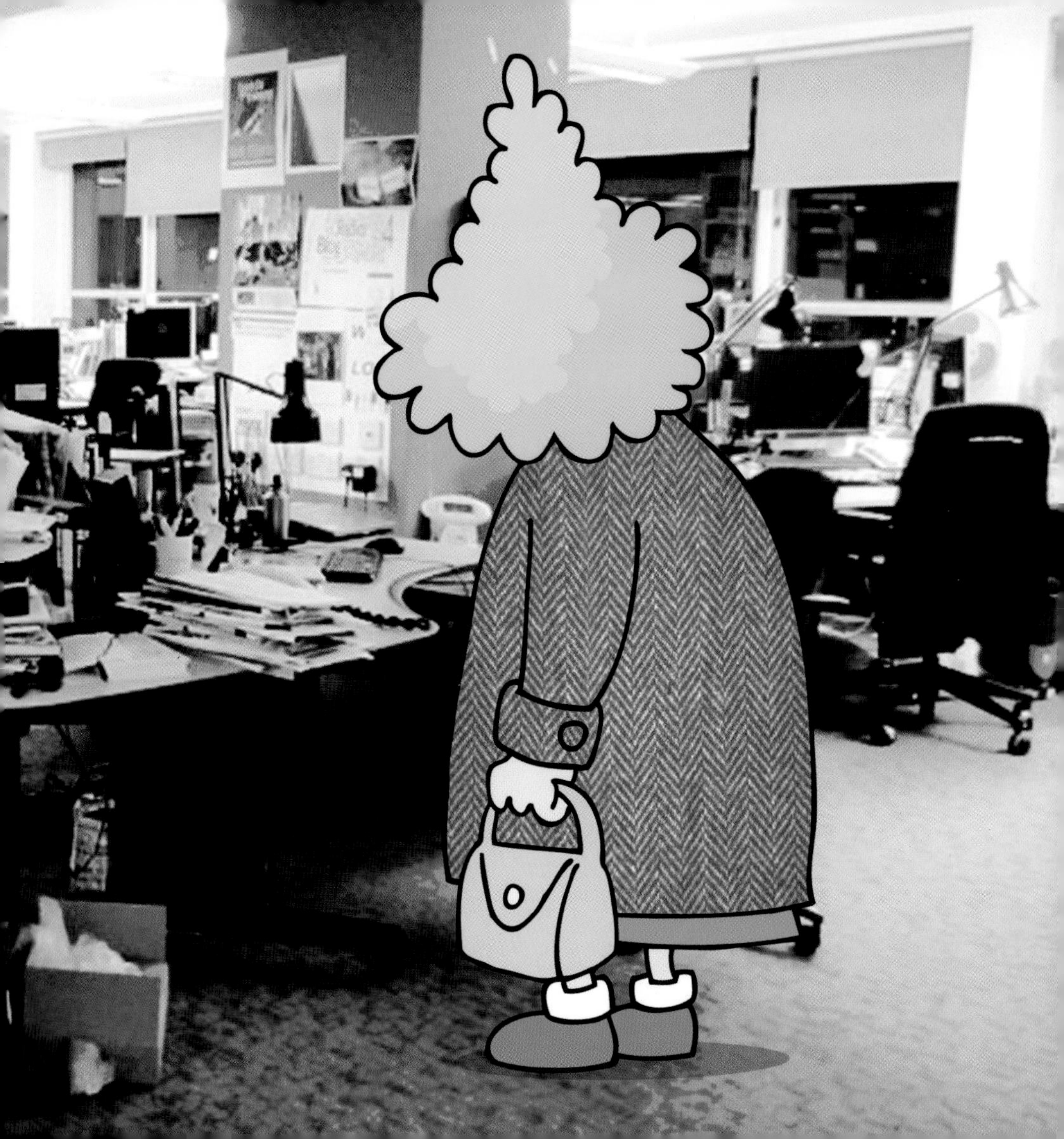

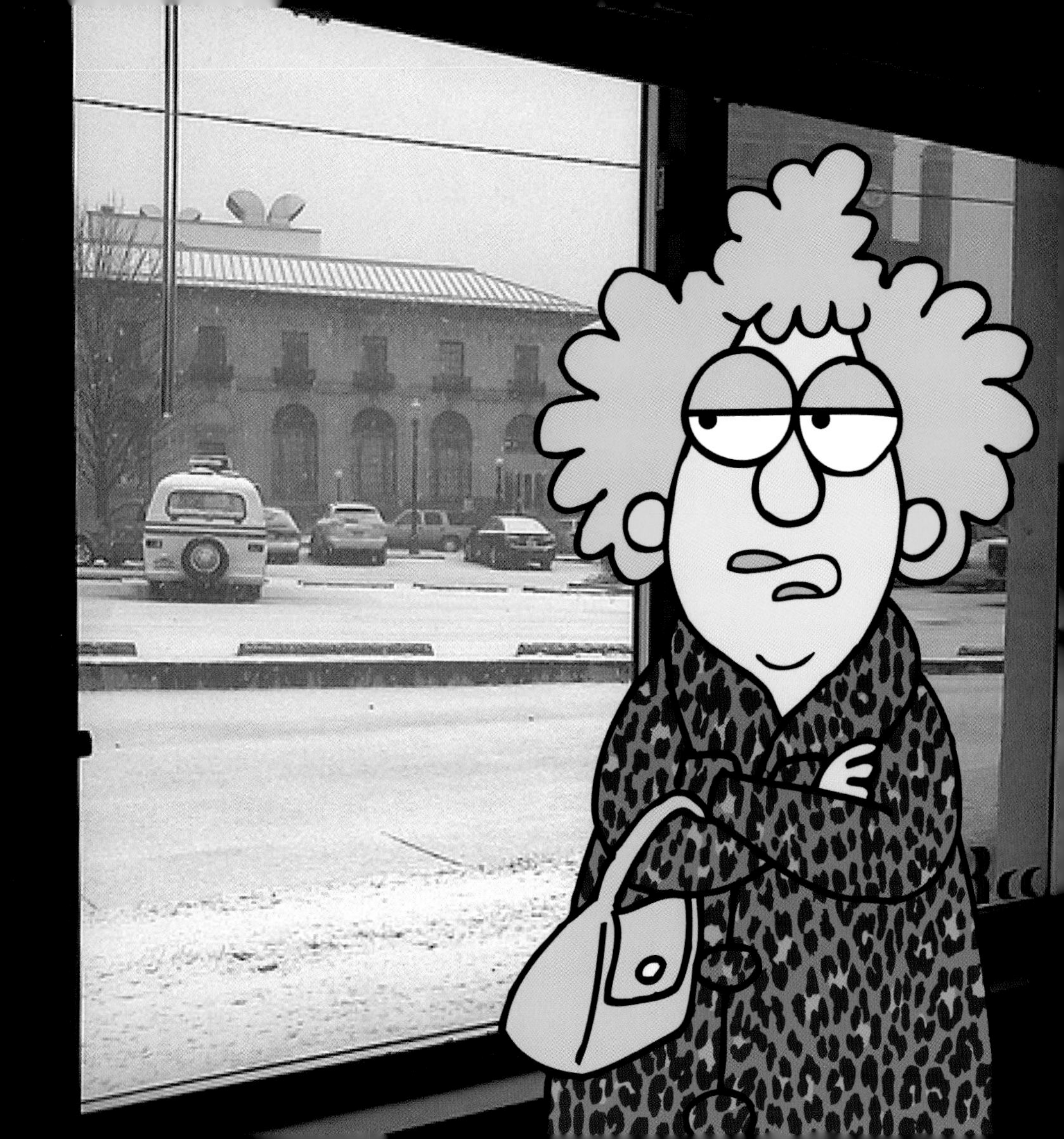

When it comes to driving to work, I have one simple rule:

If it's snowing, I'm not going.

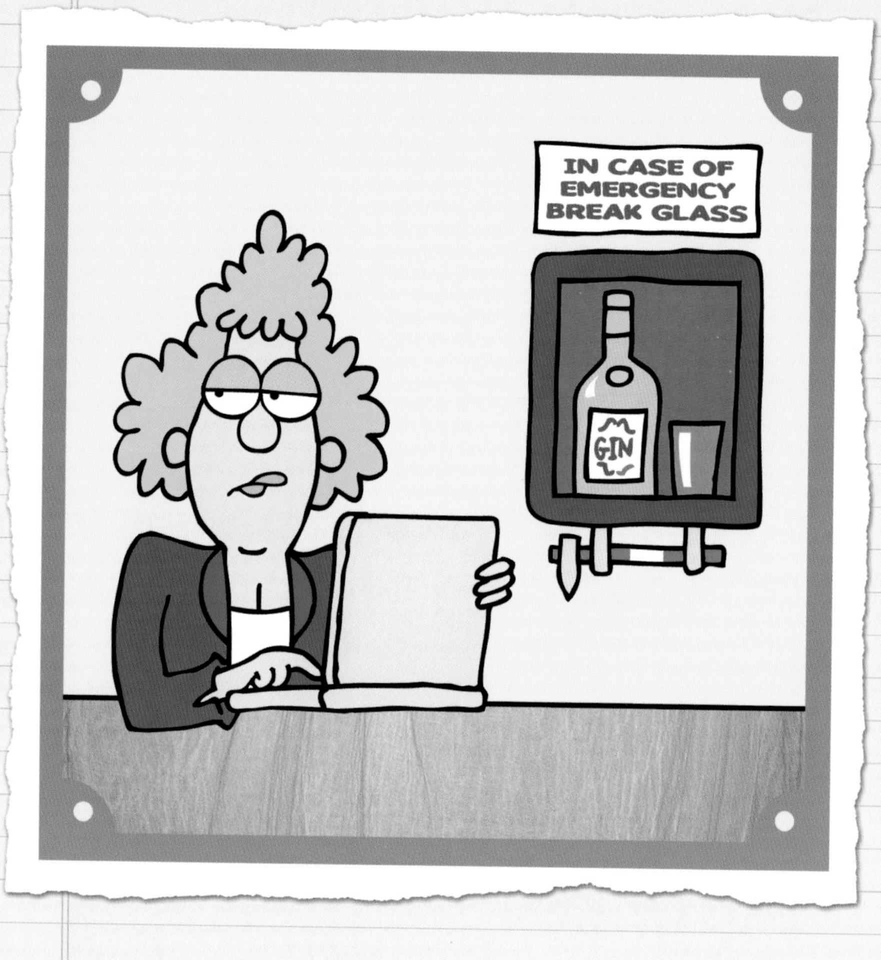
IN CASE OF
EMERGENCY
BREAK GLASS
GIN

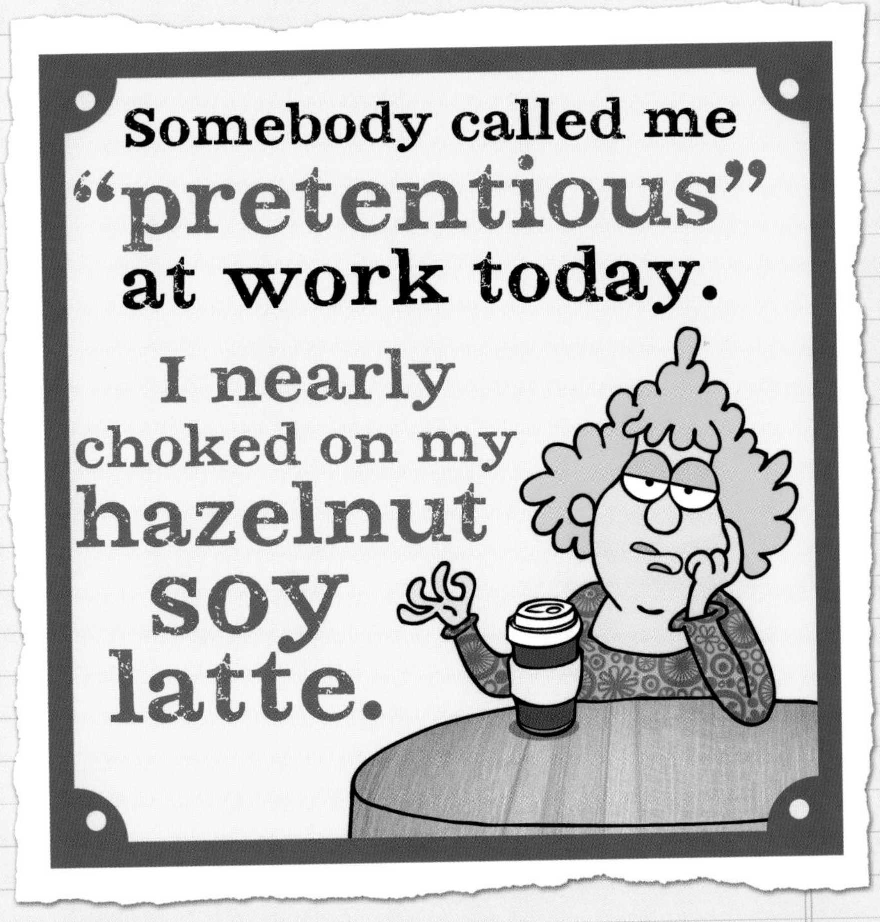
Somebody called me "pretentious" at work today.
I nearly choked on my hazelnut soy latte.

You spend the prime of your life having the stuffing beaten out of you in some soulless office; then they give you a freakin' clock as a retirement gift, so you can watch what's left of your miserable life tick away.

Go figure!

You spend the prime of your life having the stuffing beaten out of you in some soulless office; then they give you a freakin' clock as a retirement gift, so you can watch what's left of your miserable life tick away.

Go figure!

And so endeth another 8 hours praying for a power outage that never happened.

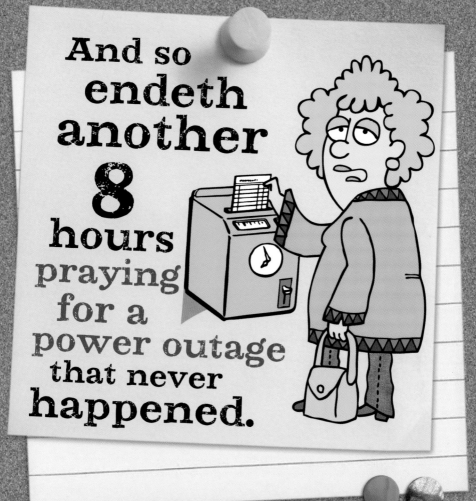

First Edition
19 18 17 16 15   5 4 3 2

Cartoons © 2015 Ged Backland

All rights reserved. No part of
this book may be reproduced by
any means whatsoever without
written permission from the
publisher, except brief portions
quoted for purpose of review.

Published by
Gibbs Smith
P.O. Box 667
Layton, Utah 84041

1.800.835.4993 orders
www.gibbs-smith.com

Illustrations by
Dave Iddon @ The Backland Studio
Designed by Dave Iddon
Contributed material by
Raychel Backland

Printed and bound in China

Gibbs Smith books are printed
on either recycled, 100% post-
consumer waste, FSC-certified
papers or on paper produced
from sustainable PEFC-certified
forest/controlled wood source.
Learn more at www.pefc.org.

ISBN 13: 978-1-4236-3968-8